Fifty Years with Father

Father and son. Black Forest. 1931

Fifty Years with Father

A Relationship

DAVID UNWIN

London
GEORGE ALLEN & UNWIN
Boston   Sydney

**George Allen & Unwin (Publishers) Ltd,
40 Museum Street, London WC1A 1LU, UK**

George Allen & Unwin (Publishers) Ltd,
Park Lane, Hemel Hempstead, Herts HP2 4TE, UK

Allen & Unwin Inc.,
9 Winchester Terrace, Winchester, Mass 01890, USA

George Allen & Unwin Australia Pty Ltd,
8 Napier Street, North Sydney, NSW 2060, Australia

First published in 1982

British Library Cataloguing in Publication Data

Unwin, David
    Fifty years with father.
1. Unwin, *Sir* Stanley 2. Unwin, David
3. Publishers and publishing – Great Britain
– Biography
I. Title
070.5′092′4   Z325.U/
ISBN 0-04-920065-8

Set in 11 on 13 Baskerville by Grove Graphics, Tring,
and printed and bound in Great Britain by
William Clowes (Beccles) Limited, Beccles and London

For my brother
RAYNER
without whose persistent encouragement
this book
would never have been written

One

My parents were married in December 1914 and made their first home on the top floor of an awesomely ugly block of late nineteenth century flats which, surviving zeppelins, the Blitz and re-development, still stands in Northwest London. Here they lived through the war years; a depressing period for them – as for most people – with hardships and rationing and the death as a baby of my elder sister.

My father, however, was not involved in the fighting. He served from an early stage in the VAD and was exempted from call-up on business grounds until 1917, when he successfully pleaded conscientious objection. Pacifists were not sympathetically handled and it is interesting to quote from a recommendation written on his behalf to the tribunal by the Minister of his Congregational Church: 'I have known Mr Stanley Unwin for some time, as I married him; and I may say with confidence that no man I have met is more sincere or genuine. What he states as his belief is his belief. And by his principles he tries to live.' Oddly expressed, perhaps, but an admirable summing up of his character.

Soon after the Armistice, my arrival added to their concerns, for I was a sickly child, nourished – if legend is to be credited – on a diet of dill water. Having already lost their first baby, it must have seemed that they were about to say goodbye to their second. I survived, but the struggle scarred them. Writing to me a score of years later, my father cannot resist reminding me what a trouble I had been. 'It really is unbelievable that you will be twenty on Saturday! How time is slipping by. You have been a very wonderful son and have more than atoned for the tribulations through which Mummy and I had to go on your account during your

1

babyhood – an experience neither of us is likely to forget.' Not perhaps the most tactful of anniversary messages, but beautifully typical. As the Minister had stressed in his recommendation, he was nothing if not sincere.

He was also a man of habit; a precise and orderly personality, always reluctant to vary or to change his ways and quick to complain, in any case of divergency, that 'the routine had gone to pot'. He had acquired the habit of regular work early, for he had left school at the age of fifteen and joined a city firm of ship and insurance brokers in the capacity of office boy. A career in publishing was not then in his sights, and indeed might never have happened had he not been sent for, a few years later, by his step-uncle, T. Fisher Unwin, and offered a post in his firm.

Although, at this early stage in my life, I could hardly be said to have had my eye on him, I can be precise about his timetable. Punctually every weekday morning after breakfast – and this included Saturdays – he would kiss my mother goodbye, put on a brown overcoat or Burberry, place a massive Homburg hat squarely upon his head, pick up a briefcase and catch a tube train to Tottenham Court Road. After a brisk stride east – it was not in his nature to dawdle – he would arrive in Museum Street, WC1. Here at Number 40, Ruskin House, he was engaged to his complete and profound satisfaction in building up the book publishing business of George Allen, which he had bought as a bankrupt concern and launched, with the addition of his own name, on 4 August 1914.

His work may have kept him thoroughly occupied but he was a man with energy to spare. 'Home life' was equally important to him. He mentions the 'strong feelings I have about the upbringing of children' in the chapter 'Purely Personal', tucked away at the end of his autobiography, published in 1960, and follows up with a short treatise on the subject, illustrated with stories from our childhood. Asked for my opinion when the book was still in typescript, I told him that I found the section embarrassing and out of place and suggested that it might be deleted. This brought the wrath of Jehovah down upon my head. He became thoroughly worked up and I felt again – as I had not felt for many years – the force of his crushing vehemence. Clearly, this was something about which he felt passionately, a side of his nature which he wished to be exposed. He was not prepared, he insisted, to be judged by the world solely as a successful publisher and business man.

My mother, who was to play later on an important part in all her children's lives, was not at her best with us when we were very young; thankful, I feel sure, to be buttressed by husband, nursemaids and later by governesses. She was not a good disciplinarian and found it difficult to keep us in order. Father remained the ultimate weapon, to be employed as a threat or, should the worst come to the worst, summoned back to the house by telephone. This would invariably happen on a Thursday afternoon, half day off for the staff, when for once she had us on our own. And up from the office he would come and peace would be restored, not by force, for he would never lift a finger to us, but by the patient and confident application of authority.

We did not stay long in our top floor flat. Soon after my sister Ruth was born, we moved up the hill to Hampstead. Here we found ourselves in semi-rural surroundings, with walled gardens about us and a view of a large sycamore tree from our nursery window. I spent an agreeable few years in that small, end of terrace house, not a great deal in my parents' company but taught and looked after from dawn to dusk by a loyal and indefatigable governess; one of the old breed, long since vanished, who dedicated herself to 'her' children and dominated their lives. Tavvy, as we called her, was totally wrapped up in our welfare. Father and Mother did not have to endure our childish prattle: instead, they were presented by her, at intervals, with handwritten booklets of our edited sayings. This was undeniably an advantage, but mitigated in my father's view by the fact that he was doomed to suffer Tavvy's conversation at the dinner table each evening, after we had been put to bed. There were many complaints made later on this score.

In the twenties, as in Constable's time, there were sheep upon the Heath and we spent happy afternoons collecting the tufts of wool clinging to the twigs of the bushes. These we teazled out and stitched the soft wads into pincushions. Blackberries were there for the picking in the autumn. When our parents went off for a summer holiday on their own and we remained at home, I would send them letters describing the activities of the caterpillars I collected (and christened) although occasionally I had a more dramatic tale to tell. Here am I writing to them at the age of seven.

MAD DOG!

'Dear Mummy and Daddy,

Thankyou very much for the postcard lichen moss and ferns, they look sweet on the Bookcase. But do you know that Tomboy has gone into a chrysalis and such a colour, too! he is red all up by his head and at his tail a big fat greeny yellow thing, and Lucy gave me a furry one too.

Mad dog! We were playing in a sand pit when suddenly we heard a terrific barking it was behind a gorse-bush and I could not see, then some people came just in front of us and there was a little dog yapping, then there was a comotion, the lady was crying and the mad dog went into the bush, and the lady came up to us and told us to go away.

Do you know that my furry (the one that Lucy gave to me) caterpillar is beginning to go into chrysalis too!'

Tavvy was firmly egalitarian and chatted to everyone: thus, we had our favourite roadman, who swept the streets in our vicinity, and who was presented each year with a home-produced Christmas card. She would take us into Hampstead village to the shops, where slipping and slithering drayhorses were frequently unable to negotiate the steep slopes of Heath Street and where, in the drapers, she once received a half-sovereign change instead of a farthing. (This was discovered with great excitement on our return home and our excellent and honest governess at once set out into the town to give it back.) And in her company on Sunday mornings, my sister and I attended the Baptist Church.

Father sometimes came with us, but more frequently he directed his steps to the Friends' Meeting House further up the hill. 'Forms and ceremonies,' he was to write later, 'are of less importance to me than the "Inner Light", and I have found myself increasingly in sympathy with the Quaker attitude to life.' His background was Congregationalist and he always maintained that he owed 'most of what is of any real value in my character to my non-conformist up-bringing'. In his youth he had suffered a surfeit of churchgoing and his enthusiasm for any form of organised worship was already on the wane. He remained, however, a firm believer in the efficacy of prayer and to the end, when in any sort of difficulty, continued to rely on his own hot line to heaven.

If our life as children was regular and contained few if any sur-prises, this at least gave us confidence. We knew where we were and we knew what to expect. The year was studded with predictable occasions. Guy Fawkes night was one of them. We were not allowed into the cramped back garden, but watched from the drawing-room window the fireworks lit for us by Father. He once contrived to set light to a box of matches in his overcoat pocket and we were treated, in addition, to a lively acrobatic display – our agile parent hopping and leaping about and slapping his thigh – which was much more entertaining to us (and left a more permanent print on our minds) than the Roman Candles and Catherine Wheels.

Every summer we would spend a few weeks at the sea; always at Thorpeness on the Suffolk coast and always in the same small bungalow with a glass verandah. Here Father joined us and we would see something of him, but not much, for at the period I am recalling he was engaged in writing *The Truth about Publishing*, the textbook which, when it came out in 1926, was to place him at one bound in an unassailable – if slightly unpopular – position as the book trade's leading pundit, and he spent many hours shut away from us, busy at his labours.

Writing a book under the same roof as one's offspring – as I was later to discover for myself – is not without its trials, and although he had the assistance of his office secretary (an honorary aunt, for she was a family friend) the disturbances must have been frequent and distracting. 'Do you remember,' my sister writes, 'the time you were having a row with Judy (my mother's old nurse, also staying with us in the tiny bungalow. How *did* we all fit in?) who was bathing you in the tin bath? You were throwing soap at her and tipping the water all over the floor. There was a hell of a racket and I got so tense in the next room that I cut the end of my tongue putting a pair of scissors in my mouth out of sheer nerves! I can still see my dress covered with blood and Auntie Jane coming to my help. She was taking dictation at the time.'

Despite his activities and my obstreperous behaviour – to say nothing of Tavvy's presence – my father must have managed to find time for me. He was a strong believer in the Jesuits' 'first seven years' and saw to it that a bond was forged between us. I was for a long time his only son – until my brother made his welcome if belated appearance – and sons were important to him. That we had grown close to each other is confirmed by a story he always loved to recount and, since I have no recollection of the incident, I will allow him to tell it once again in his own words.

> 'I was suddenly awoken from deep sleep by David, then aged eight, calling out for me, "Daddy! Daddy!" Without stopping to think, I leapt from my bunk to go to him, but then realised that I was aboard the *Olympic*, in mid-Atlantic, and that my son was hundreds of miles away. I took note of the hour and wrote to my wife to know whether our elder boy had been ill. She replied "yes", giving the date and adding that he had called out for me in the night. Allowing for the difference in time, it was at the very moment that I had been woken up and jumped out of my bunk to go to him.'

I had always enjoyed this little tale, reflecting telepathic powers on my part, and it received the *imprimatur* of print in his autobiography. To my consternation, however, I have recently discovered that it bears little relation to the facts. A letter to my mother, written on the ship's notepaper the day after the incident, reveals that my contact with my parent was visual rather than audio.

6

'The sea still keeps smooth, the weather dull and misty. The fog horn had to be sounded last night and it woke me out of my dreams. It was about 12.30 our time and 4 am Friday morning your time and I had the strange experience of seeing David's face and head less than a foot away from me as clearly as if he were there and subsequently of feeling someone tap me on the shoulder and hearing them say, "You're all right." (I had woken up with rather a start.) I have never encountered anything so realistic and the curious thing was that I continued to see David clearly for quite 30 seconds after I opened my eyes! No doubt it was due to my excellent dinner.'

About three weeks later, in a reply to my mother, he refers to the matter again : 'It certainly *was* curious about my seeing David and I felt sure something must have been happening to him at that time. There is no doubt that thought transference is a possible and real thing between people who have a strong bond of affection.'

This seems to show what a hard time a body like the Society for Psychical Research must have of it when checking and verifying such incidents, for my father – although he always loved an anecdote – was a truthful man. He would not have deliberately distorted and improved the story.

The year he sailed across the Atlantic, 1927, was the year when it was decided that I should go to school. And at this point – not, as it emerged, to my advantage – I was to win my first battle of aesthetics. There was a choice of academies. Heath Mount was close at hand; two minutes walk away up a little lane. The Hall was a bus ride distant but was much the better school. Unfortunately, the boys there wore caps and blazers of an unacceptable shade of pink and, not unnaturally, I wished to wear Heath Mount's green cap adorned with a gold lion. Since topography worked in my favour, I got my own way. I have a photograph of myself decked out in my new regalia. I am wearing also a suitably stern expression, one foot determinedly in advance, my shorts hanging well below my knees. Sliced in half by the edge of the picture can be discerned the figure of an admiring maid.

7

To my father's sorrow, his American journey took him away from home at this crucial time. He informs my mother from the *Olympic* that he has just sent me a Post Radio Telegraph to wish me well in my school career. 'I do hope he gets on all right and *much* regret that I am not at home to watch over him, though he is too independent to avail himself of outside help.' (This, as events will show, was far from true.) And from New York he writes: 'I just loved your letter telling me all about David's first day at school. I do so regret the opportunity of hearing all about it from him whilst his impressions are new.'

After an uneventful first year at Heath Mount I was promoted and found myself up against a martinet. There was no escaping him, for at my chosen school the form master took his pupils in every subject. He had an acid, sarcastic manner and he frightened me. I became more and more miserable and eventually unburdened myself at home.

That I was able to do this is a tribute to my parents' attitude. My father had often been fearful as a child, in his case particularly of the dark, and he had always been at pains to reassure me. He would leave a walking stick beside my bed at night, enabling me to thump the floor in an emergency and bring him sprinting up the stairs. (Once, when a sharp-toothed saw blade of light thrown on to the ceiling by the lamp in the street became more than I could bear, he burst into my room in answer to my summons and dispelled my fears by vigorously agitating the curtains, transforming the vicious weapon into a wobbling, harmless jelly.) So I was listened to sympathetically and a few days afterwards, to my awed amazement, was informed that my *bête-noire* had actually entered my home one night after I was asleep, invited round to have a little chat. Anxious to know their opinion of the tyrant, I was puzzled and a trifle disappointed to have him dismissed in a casual way as 'an ordinary enough young man'.

Two

The arrival of a family brings its own problems. From the frequent hints dropped when we were older, there is no question that my father felt himself deposed, ousted from the favoured position he claimed he had enjoyed before my sister and I were born. He was only half joking when he maintained that things were never again the same for him. From that moment on, *we* were of first importance in our mother's eyes and he was relegated to second place. Whether or not this was strictly true is beside the point. He felt it to be the case; felt, indeed, aggrieved about it and he did not hesitate (when did he ever hesitate?) to let us know his feelings.

Yet my mother was aware early on that this was a problem that might have to be faced. 'I wish I did not see so plainly how terribly difficult it is to be an absorbed mother and wife at the same time!' she writes to him in 1913; the year before they were married. 'Of course,' she adds – and these are my italics – '*it largely depends on your husband.*'

She had before her the example of her younger sister, who had married Gerald Brooke of the tea firm and now had a baby boy. And in considering those two charming and cultivated young women, I am led to wonder again why they should both have chosen to marry tycoons. Could it have been entirely by chance that they each selected an ambitious man, absorbed in the cut and thrust of a business career? True, my father was not yet properly launched; uncharacteristically, at that time, he had thrown everything overboard; resigning from his step-uncle's firm (the two men were temperamentally incompatible) and spending part of his savings on a journey round the world. This was not merely a pleasure jaunt, however, but involved a serious study of overseas markets; and nothing, at this point, had been settled between my parents. They were just good friends, although my father had shrewdly attached to himself her brother as a companion on his travels.

Whatever the reasons for their choice, I feel – particularly in my mother's case – that there was an element of miscalculation involved. 'I like you, to be quite honest,' she tells my father before they are engaged, 'because you are so nice to women and seem to understand them better than most men.' She did not approve of the tycoon mentality and was outspokenly critical of her brother-in-law. 'Gerald does not quite please us by his appearance, he is thin and white and very nervy, too much enthusiasm about getting rich I'm afraid! It will be a pity if he breaks up his health over anything so entirely unnecessary.' This was over-dismissive, perhaps, but then the Storrs were comfortably off. Her father Rayner, having been given a flying start by *his* parents, had amassed by the age of forty an adequate fortune and had long since retired. Skull cap on head, he was now closeted in his study, labouring doggedly on at his *magnum opus*, a concordance of *The Imitation of Christ*. In due course her brother Jack, lovable, humorous, was to while his life away in a country village, gardening, travelling and adding to his stamp collection. The two girls seem to have been more demanding. Certainly, they were ready to challenge and to tease their men. 'I think it's a great pity you couldn't have been trained as a barrister,' my mother writes in 1913. 'I get more and more convinced it was meant for your vocation, tho' I'm not at all sure it would have been good for your character!'

Father may have been kind and, up to a point, understanding, but he was bred in the biblical tradition. The man led; the woman followed. This was the order of things as laid down by the Almighty and not open to question. When I was about to marry, he took me aside to give me a piece of advice – one of the many I have listened to in my life and rejected – and I still feel uneasy when I think about it. *'Begin,'* he told me, *'as you mean to go on.'* He was expressing the true inflexibility of the patriarch.

My mother was a sun-worshipper and adored the south. As a

young woman she had enjoyed travelling in Italy – the Edwardian Italy of E. M. Forster's early novels – and she was to remember her times there nostalgically for the rest of her life. After her marriage, she hung up her Arundel prints, her Raphaels and Pinturicchios, and arranged her majolica pots, but she was seldom to see Italy again. The south, the Latin countries with their muddle, dirt and over-excitable populace were anathema to my father. He was happy in the antiseptic north; in Germany, Switzerland and Scandinavia. The Engadine was the closest he could easily bring himself to approach the land of Dante.

Up to a point, she got her way indoors. Lip service was paid to her taste. She chose the Morris coverings for the sofa and chairs. The few good pieces of furniture arrived from her family. But for all that, my father's stamp was heavy on the home and her drawing-room transformed into an extension of the office.

Physically, they were a disparate couple and invariably out of step. While one was dynamic, the other was static. Up a Swiss alp, on one of our family excursions, they would lose contact almost immediately : shortly after starting they could have communicated only by yodel. My father was much too impatient and too lively to accommodate himself to her slow pace. She had suffered an accident in her youth and had to wear a built-up shoe, but apart from this drawback her figure was plump and non-athletic, whereas he was a spare man, strong and quick on his feet, revelling in bodily activity. When I was a small boy he used to encourage me to clamp myself to one of his legs and he would swing me easily along with him. (I tried the same trick quite innocently on an older and feebler relative and can still picture his grimace of terrified alarm as he toppled wildly off-balance above me.) He was an enthusiastic tennis player and ice skater. My parents must have skated together before the Great War, but by the time I was introduced to winter sports at the age of eight my mother was already a spectator. And a spectator to his sporting activities – and to much else besides – she inevitably remained.

When my father was young his hair was smooth and neatly parted and his beard was a coppery red. But this earlier version has been wholly supplanted in my mind by the older man, with a band of greying hair brushed back on each side of a bald dome, a frost-dusted moustache and a little, grizzled, pointed beard. He was of medium height, with a head disproportionately big for his body and one shoulder lower than the other; pulled down, so we were told, by the weight of the books he carried round with him in his travelling days. He was slightly astigmatic and always wore spectacles, but these did not muffle or distort his gaze. On the contrary, his eyes blazed through them with great candour.

His interests were not wide-ranging and he did not spread himself diffusely. He had a searchlight personality; brilliance and energy focused into a concentrated, if limited, field. He exuded confidence; on meeting him this was immediately apparent. There was no escaping his alert pounces, his swift, decisive gestures; nor was it always easy to stand up against his intimidating stare.

He was the youngest of eight children, but when I was a boy my paternal grandfather was still alive. Edward Unwin did not die until he was ninety-three years old. He was a robust man, although by the time I grew familiar with his appearance – I cannot admit to ever having *known* him – he was in advanced old age. He lived in Bromley, looked after by his unmarried daughter Ella, and I picture him seated in a cosy, cluttered drawing-room full of Victoriana; his face smothered in a huge white beard. He had bright red lips and these emerged disconcertingly from the snowy cascade. They unnerved me. What with those cherry lips and all that hair, giving grandpa a kiss was something of a problem to my sister and myself. As far as we were concerned, his only other memorable feature was his explosive sneeze. The concussion was as severe as a gunshot and used to reduce us both to helpless giggles.

Amy Brockway shared the house with them. She was Ella's life-long friend and companion, a missionary's daughter, an ardent church-goer and a formidable and somewhat masculine presence. She had a deep, musical voice, was if anything more occupied with good works than my aunt, and managed at all times when we were children to make us feel we could do better if we tried. She, too, lived on into her nineties and I am convinced, in the light of what was to happen later, that all this longevity set my father a very bad example. He was intensely proud of grandpa, who had climbed to the top of the Monument in the City of London on his eightieth birthday, and who would undoubtedly have clocked up his century had he not succumbed to prostatitis, a lethal illness at that time.

I have never been able to return to Bromley without a stirring of my childhood's unease. I did not care for the place, and Ruth felt as I did. Once, when we were staying there, she shared a room with Amy and my sister was not yet asleep when this formidable adult came to bed. 'She discreetly put a huge nightie over *everything* and got out of her clothes underneath it. Then she took out hairpins – endlessly – from her plaited coils and with the last pin the coiled hair dropped heavily below her bottom like a snake. Terrifying!' The atmosphere tended to be admonitory; we never felt at home. I suspect that my eye told me it was a poor exchange for Hampstead; certainly the Municipal Gardens were not a patch on the Heath. At night, I used to enjoy the sight of the long, lit, wriggling worms of the electric trains rattling along in the black pit of the valley. Decorated texts hung on the bedroom walls. This was my father's background, for the house was a small-scale version of The Mount, the family home, replete with billiard room and conservatories, where he had grown up and which had nearly ruined Grandpa.

I have long since decided, to my own satisfaction, that Sir Stanley was Unwin only in name; he was a product of his mother's family, the active and successful Spicers. As a youth, he realised only too keenly that he was a poor relation. His baronet uncles lived in Edwardian opulence; unquestionably, they must have served as a spur to his ambition. He had inherited their characteristics, would have recognised himself in them, and I am sure that their example must have set him on course to become, if not rich and famous, for he was never to pursue money for its own sake, at least well-founded and renowned.

Although geography, for three of my uncles had settled in New Zealand, and perhaps temperament too, distanced me from most of my Unwin relatives, I had become passionately involved with my maternal grandmother and her flat, where I was a constant visitor, had become an essential ingredient in my life. There she sat, arthritic, immovable, rug over knees, a prisoner in her red velvet chair; always in the same position, facing towards the door as I entered the drawing-room. And always, as I came in, I would see her face light up, radiant with delight, while her arms opened to enfold me. Here was someone with all the time in the world to attend to me; prepared to accept me as I was, making no effort to modify or change me, but loving me uncritically for my own sake. And in return my feelings for her were overwhelming, exceeding the love I felt for either of my parents.

She shared the flat with a gentle, rather shadowy figure, her stepson, my Uncle Wilfred. (Like his father before him he, too, had retreated in early middle age from the hurly-burly of business life.) And in attendance upon them, Martha and Judy, quintessentially loyal servants, now growing old in the service of the family.

Neither of my Storr uncles was a rich man, but they were cushioned by private incomes, and what a contrast they make to my restless, ambitious, self-made father, to whom the idea of retirement was unthinkable and who was looking forward with relish to labouring until he dropped. Knowing the firm views he held on the work ethos, it is perhaps surprising that he appears to have paid so little attention to the perils of genetic influence. The odds surely were that at least one of his children would inherit Storr attitudes and opt at the first opportunity for an easy life. I must have been approaching fifty when I attended a party at which palms were being read. I was a stranger in that gathering; my life and background were unknown to the palmist. 'Hullo,' he said, flashing me a sharp look. 'I see *you've* been resting on your oars.'

My father, I sensed it even then, was not as at home as I was at my grandmother's. He must have found her difficult to control and he may well have resented her influence over my sister and myself. For a start she was much too generous and undermined his financial arrangements to such an extent that, in protest, he cut off our supply of pocket money. We did not feel the pinch. Reasonably enough in those years he had counted out our allowance in pennies,

14

but what was even sixpence a week when Granny showered us with florins and halfcrowns?

My mother had inherited the same generous disposition and would have spoilt us if she could. She was not allowed much scope for this while we were children and I think my father's rigid austerity saddened her at times. Now and then she would be driven to protest, although she did not very frequently win the battle. One skirmish I remember came many years later. I had just entered George Allen & Unwin in a junior capacity and for the first time in my life found myself earning a modest salary. As I was still a part of the family, my father proposed to deduct, at source, a weekly charge for board and lodging. To him this must have seemed a perfectly reasonable arrangement – he had a tendency to behave as if we were living on the breadline – and one, too, which would help to give me a true idea of the value of money. My mother would have none of it. Her son paying for his keep in his own home? The idea was preposterous.

I look back, then, on my grandmother's flat as a sybaritic haven; a place of relaxation and indulgence where the softer side of my nature was given an opportunity to uncurl and flower. Not that I was unhappy or thwarted in my young life. Encouragement and stimulation I had in plenty. Should I compare a visit there to entering a greenhouse on a brisk spring day?

Three

We lived no more than a modest middle-class life, yet what a number of people surrounded and supported us! While Martha and Judy soldiered on at my grandmother's, we enjoyed the services of our own shifting army of Annies and Minnies, Margerys and Dorothys, for the household always contained a resident cook, a parlourmaid and a housemaid and these were supplemented by daily staff, nursery maids and sewing women and, of course, the chars who undertook the heavy work. Tavvy continued with us, there was a nurse for my young brother, and now, in addition, Mr Hutchinson arrived upon the scene.

I had need of a tutor, for I was always ill. I was making such a habit of illness by this time that my father must have wondered when, if ever, I was going to be educated. Not for me the odd three or four days off school, recovering from a cold. Already, I was operating on a grand scale. My complaints were so deep-rooted, so stubborn that months rather than weeks – even entire school terms – would go by while I struggled to regain my health. Nor did I lack company, for my mother's health, too, was equally precarious. Pneumonia was the cause of it all and our lungs had been affected; as a result, in the absence of antibiotics, we were able to live for long periods a delightful, detached life together in a comfortable hotel in Switzerland.

This, of course, was a very satisfactory state of affairs indeed. I was by no means miserably ill, nor, I am sure, was my mother; putting her feet up on a sunny balcony was her idea of bliss. For my part, while it was irksome to have to keep quiet for hours at a stretch, I soon recovered wind enough to take quite long walks, which my indulgent mother permitted me to do. And we were free, gloriously free. We had very cleverly contrived, the two of us, to escape from some of life's more tiresome aspects: school routine, domestic management, my father's demanding presence. Mother never really enjoyed running a house. The maids were always a worry; she was not good at handling staff. Now the place could tick over without her; my father would be fed and his wants seen to and Tavvy was there in the nursery with my brother and sister. What was more, everyone was sympathetic; everyone understood.

Father had first arrived in Lenzerheide in 1909, when the village was hardly more than a staging post on the road from Chur to St Moritz. Twenty years later it had become a resort, although ski-lifts, mountaintop restaurants, an ice-rink pavilion with music and a rash of villas speckling the lower slopes were still many seasons away. I must have spent as much time there, between the ages of nine and eleven, as I spent in Hampstead and, until the outbreak of the Second World War snapped the connection, I returned with my family every year. The Hotel Lenzerhorn became my other home.

I think it is true to say that tennis and winter sports – by which I mean skating – were my father's sole indulgences. (He puts forward the claim in his autobiography that his personal expenditure, other than on travel, was probably less than some members of his staff spent on cigarettes. I need hardly add that he was a non-smoker and a teetotaller!) And since his pleasures, as with every one of his life's activities, were taken very seriously, my sister and I came in for a great deal of assiduous coaching.

We responded – we had no choice in the matter – and we became quite nimble performers, but we were not as grateful as we might have been for our noses were kept much too close to the grindstone. The phrase 'enough is enough' had absolutely no meaning for my father. He overdid things; he never knew when to stop. I see us, then, immediately after the post-breakfast pause for essential morning duties, following him out into the intense breath of early cold; the January sun low in the sky, the rink gleaming ahead of us like polished marble, still flawless, not a scratch upon its surface. To be the first on the ice was important, because only then could we clearly mark out our eights. We were about to enter a private world of inside and outside edges, threes and drop threes, rockers and counters, brackets and loops. Round and round we circled, tracing our disciplined figures, while the sun grew warmer and other more fortunate children whirled past us with cheerful shouts on their senseless, disorderly perambulations. We would be released eventually, to enjoy ourselves in our own fashion, and Father would wind up the portable gramophone, capture the nearest available damsel and revolve gracefully in a waltz or a foxtrot, careful always to keep within earshot of the thin strains of 'Bye Bye Blackbird' or 'Valencia'. And after sundown, when the bitter cold descended and we were all indoors, he did not even then relax but set out energetically to din a few more phrases of German into my head. Always emphatic, his lessons were far from sedentary. *'Ich stehe auf,'* he would cry. *'Ich setze mich,'* bouncing up and down to suit action to the words. Then, striding across the room. *'Ich gehe nach die Tür.'*

This, I hope, gives an idea of a normal winter holiday when Father was in charge of us and we were subject (for our own good) to a regime of organised activity. What a contrast were the long quiet months of convalescence, when I was handed over to my mother's care. An extraordinary calm descended. Pressures were removed. I was at liberty and I could be myself; no longer distracted by that busy dynamo now humming harmlessly in London, hundreds of miles away.

I began to live through my eyes. I became fascinated by the personalities of the peaks with which I was surrounded. As I explored further afield, I found that their shapes altered and that, as a result, their characters curiously changed. These mountains grew into my being and I never tired of observing their varying shapes and moods. Staying in Lenzerheide for as long as I did, I saw out the normal season for visitors. I witnessed the dramatic changes when spring arrived and the shining icing-sugar slopes became blotched and disfigured with patches of brown, as if my friends were suffering from some hideous skin disease; and I watched with dismay the tidy, frozen surface of the village street disintegrate into chaotic ruts and runnels, revealing the earth beneath, muddy and wet. I returned in the summer, to find that my white world had changed into a green world, drab and matt by comparison, disappointingly lacking in dazzle and brilliance. The sledges had gone, replaced by wheeled wooden carts, although the valley still echoed to the crack of the drivers' whips.

I had, of course, no glimmer of a suspicion of what was happening to me on these solitary excursions. They were a jolt to my senses, a necessary awakening, but more than this; they signal an emergence, an arrival. I was becoming my own person. I had begun to change, to grow away from my father, to turn into someone of whom he could not be expected to approve. This is all hidden as yet and far ahead; something that would not be understood for many years.

Four

Our birthdays were always occasions – to borrow one of my father's phrases – for 'gatherings of the clan'. Uncles, aunts and cousins were invited to tea and afterwards grouped themselves at each side of the folding table on which presents were laid, hidden until opening time under a bright Swiss scarf. The string round the parcels was never allowed to be cut; knots were unpicked and the lengths neatly tied up again and placed in the bag designed to hold them. The ritual did not vary as we grew older, but the thinning ranks of our relatives and their increasing decrepitude marked the passage of time.

We were still in Hampstead but were residing in Oak Hill Park; at that time a private estate of substantial semi-detached houses with its own mews, gates and entrance lodge. This move, which took place when I was nine or ten years old, transformed our lives. For a rent of £110 p.a. we now had a larger home and two gardens, one attached to the house, and the second, the Old Garden, which covered nearly half an acre, lying at the top of the estate. And on this piece of land my father instantly built himself a tennis court.

My parents were to live at Number Four for more than thirty years and during that period remarkably little changed. Once the furniture had been set in place, the pictures hung, the books – and there were quantities of them to add to the annual labour of spring cleaning – arranged in precise order on the shelves built for them to my father's design (boot lockers below; Martin-ware pots on top), the rooms ossified. Light fittings had always been one of his pet economies and they moved with us once again, some of them cumbersome contraptions with weights and cables, already venerable in the late twenties. They were so much a part of my life, I had for so long ceased to notice them, that it was only much later, in the fifties, when friends of ours first glimpsed the house with amazed delight, that I realised what a museum the place had become. A few gadgets were reluctantly updated, but for years we hung on to our crystal wireless set with headphones. And very practical these were for listening unobtrusively in bed; Henry Hall was my constant pillow companion.

The move accomplished, Father adjusted to his changed surroundings and settled down into the diurnal rhythm he enjoyed and from which he was always reluctant to deviate. As before, his were the group of coat hooks nearest the front door, and woe betide the unwary visitor who might usurp them. (We, of course, knew better.) In the drawing-room he had taken possession of a small boudoir armchair of my mother's and of the delicate mahogany table that stood beside it, on the polished top of which he piled each evening an unsuitably heavy weight of papers, manuscripts and books. His entrance into the hall between halfpast six and seven – for he seldom left the office punctually – was always a cheerful event, and if I was within earshot the slide and click of his key in the lock would bring me rushing out to greet him; not entirely for the pleasure of his company, although I loved him warmly, but for the excitement of finding out what he had brought back for me. His bulging briefcase invariably held some little treat in the shape of foreign stamps or cigarette cards (these last, of course, cadged on my behalf from colleagues who smoked) or perhaps a children's book.

At this period of my life I ate my supper in my bedroom (brought up on a tray by the housemaid) but I was soon to grow familiar with the adult downstairs ritual and can report upon it with confidence, for it never varied. After an early meal – punctuality was of the essence, for my teetotal father could not dally at this point with a sustaining drink – he would open *The Times* – the *News Chronicle* was his breakfast reading – and the silence would remain unbroken until, with a rustle and a grunt, he collapsed the pages and beat them into shape, before hurling the paper across the room to my mother, who sat opposite him on the sofa at the other side of the fireplace. His manuscripts would occupy him until nine, when there was an interval for the news, after which he would return to them

21

until about ten o'clock. Soon afterwards, he would be on his way to bed.

His work put him in touch with many interesting people, for at this period he was publishing books by Bertrand Russell, Laski, Lowes Dickinson, Aldington and Čapek, to name only a few of the more famous, but he saw them in the office or at his club. Authors were absent from our table and we did not meet any book trade figures. His fellow publishers were not entertained at home. (My father now found himself living immediately opposite Geoffrey Faber but, although the two men were in frequent correspondence, I doubt if they crossed each other's thresholds.) This was not surprising, for my parents entertained to a very limited extent. Here he is, in what appears to be a sort of apologia, putting it down to the absence of drink.

> 'My wife and I have never been particularly interested in social activities outside our respective family circles. For one thing we followed my parents in having nothing alcoholic in the house, which limited our guests to those who would not find that too great a deprivation. Most of my business entertaining has always been done at my club, where my guests suffer no such limitations.'

How blandly he links my mother in with him! Yet she was not by nature abstemious and she was not brought up a teetotaller; indeed, she came from a relaxed and convivial home. She was prepared, however, to bow to his wishes and she waited uncomplainingly until her late middle-age, by which time he had mellowed sufficiently to permit her a small glass of wine at mealtimes, on her doctor's recommendation and strictly on medicinal grounds.

She would not have felt this a serious sacrifice, but she was called upon to make others. Before she married, she had been a sociable being and her early letters are filled with descriptions of groups and gatherings and reveal her lively interest in her fellow humans, an interest my father not only did not share but, already in 1913, was doing his best to suppress.

'I agree with you,' she writes, 'that gossip is a curse. I am afraid you will have no more to say to me after the last letter I wrote. I *do* pull people to pieces I'm afraid, not because I wish to appear clever but because I find them so uncommonly interesting, especially their funny little ways. I know *my* bones are picked in return! I will try and be better in future.' And again : 'Between ourselves, surely the Luke ménage is a funny one? Your description of the household was really rather humorous, tho' you probably did not realise it! You might have mentioned the housekeeper, I think!!'

How lovingly she teases him, pointing out that he has missed the – human – point.

Why did she so markedly lose her assurance, her social poise? For change she did, in the most regrettable way. From hints dropped when I was growing up, I have an idea that their early attempts, during the war years, to give an occasional dinner party, had ended badly. Whatever it was that went wrong, my mother's confidence seems to have been permanently undermined. I never knew the empirical young woman, eager to test herself and take on responsibilities. 'My great ambition is to run the house entirely for six months and give Mother a perfect rest from housekeeping which she badly wants,' she asserts before her wedding, and she tells my father that 'if marriage means devoting oneself to one man only and giving up all my friends, I think I shall prefer single blessedness.' Twenty-five years later, when she reveals 'a bit of her soul' to a close friend, she is saddeningly unrecognisable. 'I believe if Stanley had not got a stupid and retiring wife he would rise to great heights. It's often worried me and still does sometimes how much of a drag on his social life I really am.'

(I suspect that she had in mind formal Book Trade occasions, for Father was an enthusiastic Congress-goer. Conventional sociabilities, unconnected with his work or his family, he invariably regarded as a waste of time.)

The visitors from the world outside who *did* appear in our midst, apart, of course, from our relatives, were a distinctly mixed bunch.

23

This is not surprising, in view of the fact that they had been singled out not for their wit, grace or learning, although a few possessed these qualities, but for their backhands and volleys. I refer to the tennis players. Regularly as clockwork, these arrived in their white flannels at two o'clock on Saturday and Sunday afternoons and were later entertained in the drawing-room where, in my mother's company and with the dust and sweat of battle still clinging to their bodies, they slaked their thirst from shallow Copenhagen tea cups and restored their energies with cucumber standwiches and a slice or two of cake. On fine summer days these 'tennis teas' took place in the Old Garden. Chairs and tables would be arranged outside the wooden summer-house which overlooked the court and a procession of maids with flushed faces, carrying kettles and heavy baskets, would wend its way up the hill from the house. The great Drobny himself once played in one of my father's fours, and Dr Joad was a frequent performer. The organisation of the matches was shared by his secretary, and last-minute cancellations gave rise to frantic bouts on the telephone. Father played winter and summer, year in, year out, impervious to cold, fog or drizzle. Always optimistic, however foul the weather, he would give no quarter to the weaker spirits who rang up before the match, transparently hoping to be released from the ordeal.

His pursuits were all active. He was not a collector, except possibly of books. Fresh books certainly continued to arrive in the house, but these were either gifts or recent publications of Allen & Unwin. Seldom if ever would he buy a book from a bookshop. He was too keenly occupied in *selling* them his wares. His mother, whom he revered, had taught him as a boy to do without; the most valuable lesson in his life, he maintained. He did not consider it a hardship or a limitation to make himself independent of material things. Not having suffered family privation, it is easy enough for me to take an opposite stance. I have always found pleasure in surrounding myself with interesting and beautiful possessions. Already, at ten years old, I was becoming a magpie and, in an uninformed, boyish way, collecting everything I could : stamps, cigarette cards, shells and fossils, butterflies, birds' feathers, foreign coins . . . Unfortunately, soon after we moved to Oak Hill Park, my magpie instinct got badly out of hand. I have reached perhaps the most bizarre incident of my childhood and one which was to cause my poor father and mother the maximum of embarrassment and concern.

The crisis came at a weekend, after tennis was over, for Father was reading aloud to us in the drawing-room. My sister and I were sitting together on the sofa, side by side. I cannot now recall the story; perhaps it was Kipling's 'Baa Baa Black Sheep', always a favourite of his. Suddenly, the door opened and in came my mother, her face stern, holding a small brown notebook in her hand. 'I want to know the meaning of this,' was all she said, but it was enough. I felt my spine prickle and Ruth instantly subsided into tears. However, I ran across the room and tried to urge my more malleable parent out into the hall. I felt that all might still be saved if I could get her away, explain to her on her own. But Father was already involved; it was too late; we had to confess.

We had been raiding handbags. Either because few if any of our lady guests smoked or made up their faces, or perhaps because it was the custom of the times, bags were almost always left with coats and hats in the hall. Spying from the landing above, we would wait until the guests were safely in the drawing-room; then we would swoop like a pair of hawks upon our prey. We were restrained, in that we only took a single coin from each bag; one coin was our rule, no more, but preferably a large one. Then, after stashing away the loot, I would make a careful record of the transaction in my notebook. Date, name and amount. And my mother, of course, observed me scribbling in my little brown book and her lively bump of curiosity led her in the end, as I should have known it would, to look inside and discover what I was up to. I had made no attempt to hide it but had left it lying about.

Our biggest haul must have been the most shaming to my father. He had invited all the girls in the office up to tea and to enjoy the banks of bluebells in the Old Garden. A dozen typists and secretaries deposited a small mountain of handbags upon the hall table. A jackpot! Peering down from the heights, we could hardly credit our luck. Later, when the game was up, I faced the terrifying possibility that I might have to go down to Museum Street and apologise personally to them all. This hung over my head for a while, but in the end my father let me off and, as he was to do so often in my life, shouldered the burden for me. The girls were sympathetic and understanding and, to comfort him, one of them told him that her brother had also stolen when a boy.

We did not need the money and we made no use of it. Our stealing was really a form of thoroughly dishonest collecting, for we left the hoard intact. There it all was, neatly stowed away in a black japanned cash box hidden among the roots of one of the elm trees in the garden. And, thanks to my notebook, it could all be paid back. On reflection a curious escapade, in which I was the ring-leader, the master mind. I may have acted acquisitively, but I am sure also that I was in search of excitement, for I was at a loose end still and not yet back at school.

Five

I had earlier said goodbye to Heath Mount and, when the doctors decided that I was strong enough to lead a normal life, I resumed my scholastic career, wearing this time the despised pink cap and blazer of The Hall. And I soon made my mark there by becoming the only boy in the school who refused to wear a tie. Why I was allowed to get away with it in those conservative pre-war days I shall never understand. However, the headmaster was a liberal man and my parents, I know, raised no objection.

Father was always on the side of dress reform, loathed dinner jackets, refused steadfastly to change for dinner in hotels where it was the custom to do so, and seized every possible holiday occasion to spread an open-necked shirt over the collar of his Norfolk jacket. A neat man, his appearance was never quite *smooth*, although he had his suits made for him by a Bond Street tailor. By the time clothes rationing arrived he must have accumulated a sufficient wardrobe to see him through, which was helpful to the family, for we were able to use his coupons. And at some stage in the war he must have decided not to wear a hat. From a hatted publisher, he was transformed overnight into a hatless publisher, and bare-headed he remained until the end of his life. His walking shoes were marvellously blunt and unstylish, designed expressly to give ample freedom to his toes. The fact that he wore each of his suits, on and off, for thirty or forty years – he never succumbed to middle-age spread; indeed, his figure altered very little – may have accounted at times for their slightly bulgy appearance, but I would put most of the blame on the load he carried in his pockets.

His waistcoats, in particular, were a source of interest to us as children. When we knocked up with him on the tennis court on weekday evenings, he would shed this clinking, rattling garment, which weighed in the hand as heavily as a piece of chain mail, encumbered as it was with all the invaluable gadgets from which he never wished to be parted. His bunch of keys was a weapon in itself; his alarm watch a thick and solid affair. The Boy Scout side of his nature found expression in a pair of blunt-nosed scissors and a twin-bladed penknife, but his equipment also included two dainty little, rather feminine, mother-of-pearl objects, one a nail cleaner and the other a paper knife. They looked much the same to us but were fortunately quite distinct in *his* mind, for the larger he often used for peeling fruit, while with the smaller he not only cleaned his nails but, with the blunt end, used to dig the wax out of his ears. Having observed him perform these various operations, when offered a slice of peeled peach or apple we would tease him by shrinking away in simulated horror and disgust. (My sister was very good at this.) He never failed to rise; indignantly fishing in a separate waistcoat pocket and holding up the two little nacreous appliances, one in each hand, for comparison.

*

He continued to encourage me with my German – not taught at my preparatory school – and he promised to take me on a trip abroad with him; but on one condition. After we crossed the Rhine, I must not talk a word of English. *Ich muss nur Deutsch sprechen!* I accepted the challenge and we went on the first of these walking tours in 1931, when I was twelve years old. I was tongue-tied for the first day or two but managed fairly quickly to find a stumbling German voice. Then a difficulty arose, for my father (correctly) was addressing me in the '*du*' form, used by adults to children, and I was picking this up and using it myself when talking to grown-ups. This would not do, so he altered his technique and started to address me as '*sie*'. Soon afterwards, he was approached by a German guest at the hotel, who had overheard our conversation in the dining-room. Who was the little boy? he enquired respectfully. A prince?

He took me on three of these holidays in successive years, and they highlighted the preferential treatment I was enjoying as his elder son. My brother was still too young, but in spite of the fact that his adored mother had had strong feelings about equality of the sexes, he very unfairly never considered giving Ruth this sort of chance. There was no genuine democracy in our family and all through our childhood my sister came off second best.

I brought back from those walking tours happy memories of forests and castles, Camberwell Beauty butterflies flaunting their purple outside my bedroom window, trout netted from the stream beside the wayside restaurant; plenty of good fare and an appetite to match it. My father shared my schoolboy dislike of sour tasting things and my eagerness for sweets; he amused the waiters by telling them that we liked our lettuce *'wie die Kaninchen fressen'* – as rabbits eat it, or in other words, undressed. We carried rucksacks and bought ourselves walking sticks. There was a vogue then for *Stocknägel*, little stamped tin mementoes of the places you passed through and which you attached to your stick. My father contented himself with one, but my collector's fervour got the better of me and my stumpier stick was soon glittering with them from handle to ferrule. On our second visit the presence of the Nazi party was making itself felt and political signs and slogans were daubed everywhere. Father already sensed danger ahead. Although he had the warmest admiration – and love – for the German people, he was revolted by the Nazis and all they stood for and we spent a lot of time diligently scrawling the three arrows of the Social Democrat party across the menacing image of the swastika. We got on extremely well together. I had not yet begun to feel in any degree critical; on the contrary I looked up to him and loved him warmly and he, I think, may have found me a responsive and eager companion. But I could have hoped, perhaps, as the days went by, that he would become a little less insistently concerned with the state of my bowels.

This was an obsession of his, an inheritance from the fears of the previous century, and the dangers of constipation soon dominated my thoughts to such a extent that I made up a long poem on the subject – I am ashamed to say, in English! – a Belloc-influenced cautionary tale which ended with the mortally-constipated young hero lying beneath a marble tombstone 'topped by a marble po'. I contrived an illustrated version in different coloured inks on my return to Hampstead, which I hung in the downstairs loo, but it was not well received and permitted only a brief viewing.

Home again, I was entering the period when my father's bed-time goodnights began to extend themselves into regular prayer sessions. These grew longer and longer until at times, and I think to my mother's slight impatience, they ran into and even beyond the sacred supper hour. He has described his own father's interminable extempore praying, when it seemed to the young Stanley that there was no reason why he should *ever* stop; but family prayers at The Mount were formal occasions, with everyone present, servants included, and all of them no doubt kneeling uncomfortably on a hard floor. Whereas I was lying snugly with my head on the pillow, my father sitting on the edge of the bed and holding my hand, and all I had to do was to close my eyes (which I was about to do very soon in any case) and absorb his eminently reasonable monologue with God. And since my father's prayers were largely concerned with my spiritual and moral welfare, they put me where every child always longs to be anyway, at the centre of the stage, enjoying the individual and exclusive attention of one or other parent.

We would begin informally, by chatting about stamps, perhaps, or he would ask me what I had been doing at school. We would approach the serious business of the evening by way of an anecdote, of which he had a store, and heartening tales these were, for they concerned dramatic personal interventions made by the Almighty on behalf of Stanley Unwin. On many occasions during his life, when my father had found himself in a tight corner, a prayer prayed in the nick of time had apparently done the trick. I loved these stories and when I was a boy never tired of hearing them re-peated – which, I need hardly add, they frequently were. I cannot refrain from giving a typical example.

Once, on a cold and wet and windy night, my father was bi-cycling across Germany. He was trying to find a country boarding school, his destination, but he had lost his way in a land of endless fir trees. The forests were without landmarks, there was nothing to guide him, and he was pedalling on rather desperately through the darkness, wondering what to do. So he sent up a prayer, a heartfelt prayer, for advice, for rescue, and immediately – *psscht!* A puncture. A flat tyre. He was brought to a juddering halt.

A dirty trick of the Almighty's? His troubles compounded? Not a bit of it. As he stepped off his crippled machine, my father saw a light. Over there in the black wilderness a light twinkled, beckoning to him, a ray of hope. A light, in fact, that turned out to come from the school. But that was not all. Next day, he retraced his steps and discovered that his puncture had occurred at the one and only point on the road from which the buildings of the school could be glimpsed through the trees. If God – and the puncture – had not stopped him in his tracks at that exact spot he would have ridden by.

I found these sessions with him snug and reassuring. To my sister however, who had the same prayer treatment, they were embarrassing and unacceptable. She could not bring herself to believe that they were genuine. (She reacted in much the same way to his over-sentimental side, which she felt to be unnatural and, hence, acutely painful to her.)

If spiritual aspects were important, the physical side of things must not be ignored. Now that I was growing up, an event loomed in my life. Hints were solemnly dropped. The initiation that lay ahead was too important to be rushed into in a hurry and certainly could not be fitted into any casual slot of time. Nor, I gathered, could the subject be raised in Hampstead; even the privacy of my own bedroom was not deemed sufficient. I must be removed altogether from the turmoil of family life and taken to some tranquil place where, in a suitably serene atmosphere, I might prepare myself for the revelation. Father was about to inform me of the facts of life.

That was his plan and we travelled down together, one weekend, to spend a night in a house in the country. I have no idea why he had chosen to stay with these particular people, but for the purpose of his visit the choice of location seems comically apt. For in the house lived one of the many missionaries' daughters brought up with the Unwin family, married now and a buxom and fertile mother of an immense number of children. They were of all sizes and ages and they swarmed everywhere. We should have been much more peaceful at home.

However, we withdrew eventually and he did spend his long-promised evening with me upstairs – had he, I wonder, informed them of what he was up to? – and we worked our way rather ploddingly through bees and birds and bovines to the inevitable crunch moment, the shock of which must have woken me up, for I remember it to this day. 'You do *that*?' On reflection, it still seems to me a very odd arrangement.

My father and I were never to be so close as in those years of the early thirties. As I grew older, inevitably my viewpoint would alter and I would begin to find myself in conflict with many of his sincerely felt and strongly held beliefs. We may have had a stormy time waiting for us, but for the moment all was going well. We were sailing calmly forward on a halcyon sea.

Six

'My dear David,

I hated parting with you today. The holidays have been wonderful but they seem to have gone like a flash.

Somehow I don't seem to have had as much of you to myself as sometimes and I have been much too pre-occupied. It was rotten luck having the job of President of the Publishers' Association thrust upon me again owing to Mr Taylor's illness.

However I hope someday to be a little more free, but it won't be till after the International Publishers Congress – possibly not until April of next year when my Vice Presidency comes to an end.

Meanwhile you are I imagine happily settled down at Abbotsholme again. It is a wonderful life there in wonderful country and you must make the most of it.

You will have increased responsibility and increased work but neither will hurt if taken in the right spirit. On the contrary both help to prepare you for what is ahead. Self discipline is the best discipline and that is what responsibility calls for. The lack of power to concentrate seems to me one of the great failings of the age. There is no excuse for it. It is merely lack of effort or lack of guts!

Well, I have the completest confidence in you that any father ever had in any son and with more justification than many, because I know that you are incapable of letting me down.

You are a dear!

God bless you!

Ever your devoted Daddy

Stanley Unwin.'

I have jumped forward a few years. It is now January 1936 and my father is writing to me at my public school. His opening letter of the term was often an exhortation, a clarion call urging me forward into the battle of life, and this one is no exception. In an ingenious way, he is also at pains to emphasise how occupied he is, and to let me know what an important book trade figure he has now become. But the final paragraph does worry me for, apart from moral blackmail, it reveals that he is not really aware of me as an individual. I am becoming a stereotype. He is writing to me, not as I am but what he wants me to be, a paragon son. This may be an easy mistake for a busy parent to make, but it is bound to lead to trouble. Of course I was going to let him down.

Abbotsholme was a fairly odd place when I arrived there in the summer of 1933, but in my father's day it must have been odder still, particularly in the context of those rather stuffier times. My Uncle Sidney was one of the first three boys at the school and he and my carpenter uncle, Bernard, returned to teach there. Both these men suffered mental breakdowns in their later lives, and my father laid the blame for their misfortunes squarely upon the founder and headmaster's 'hypnotic influence'. (Not surprisingly, in view of this, Dr Cecil Reddie occupied pole position in his demonology.) Right or wrong, this was his conviction, and like all my father's convictions, firmly held. He himself, he always assured me, had 'seen through him'. Certainly he proved, even as a boy, to be more than a match for the Head's overpowering and dominant personality.

The question, then, might fairly be asked, why did he risk sending his sons to Abbotsholme? But the Abbotsholme of the thirties was an entirely new venture, although organised along somewhat similar lines. The school under Dr Reddie had suffered a sad decline in later years and was eventually forced to close down. At this point, a group of dedicated Old Boys came to the rescue, my father among them; took charge and installed another Head. Thus it was that, in company with a coach load of assorted boys dressed in the same outlandish uniform – heather tweed knickerbocker suits, the coats with large round leather buttons, berets, woollen stockings and sensible brown shoes – I steamed out of St Pancras station one afternoon en route for Derbyshire and a bracing boarding school life on the banks of the River Dove.

I had always been called 'onion' at The Hall; now I found that my name came as no surprise to anyone. I was Unwin 9, Unwins 7 and 8 were in the forms above and below me, while Uncle Bernard was back on the staff again in charge of woodwork. (This was awkward for us both, since he was a dedicated craftsman and I had no aptitude for carpentry, and was as likely as not to pick up a chisel and use it as a screwdriver.) Our Head was a benign giant, his wife taught classics and their children, although not our fellow pupils, had their home with us. A reassuring family group they made, and a necessary one, for Dr Reddie had never married and his quirky bachelor imprint was still strong upon the school.

All about us, in chapel, hall and dining-room, were representations of the naked – masculine – body. I took them for granted and never gave them much thought. They came as no revelation, for the naked bodies of my schoolfellows were all about me anyway, in the showers and when we were swimming in the river. Only after I had left Abbotsholme did it gradually dawn on me that the décor was, perhaps, a little queer.

The chapel, for example, was dominated by a larger-than-life figure of a splendidly developed young man carved out of white marble. He was modelled, so it was rumoured, on a past Head Boy. Conceived as a War Memorial and inspired by Blake's design, the Radiant Lover stood on tiptoe, chest lifted and arms spread wide, in bold relief against a background of marble rays. Blue velvet curtains concealed him, but at times of religious observance these were drawn aside, when he instantly became the focus of attention; our altar-piece, in fact, for there was no other. He was an inescapable element in every service we attended. Hymns, prayers and the periodic chanting of the school song with its rousing chorus – *For the love, the love of comrades* – have become inextricably entwined in my mind with this over-sized youngster's tiptoe, ecstatic stance and his prominent private parts.

There were other quaint aspects to Abbotsholme, left-overs from

35

the past. I never became reconciled to the earth cabinets – or cabs as they were called – although they would find favour today with the ecologists. A row of primitive wooden cubicles equipped with shovels and boxes, they stood across the yard at a convenient distance from the (thriving) kitchen garden which supplied the school with vegetables. There were about ten or a dozen of them and five or six boys shared a cab, for Abbotsholme was only just beginning to build up its numbers. The staff, unfairly we used to think on frosty winter mornings, had their own conventional water closets inside the main building. Using these was against the rules, but I sometimes risked it for the relief, the inexpressible pleasure, of finding myself supported once again on a properly-shaped seat and no longer squatting uncomfortably over a draughty void. Father, however, was an enthusiast for the cabs and made a point of inspecting them on his visits to the school. I have heard him declare more than once that in *his* day they were kept so clean that 'you could eat an apple off the floor'. I have pondered over this statement since and asked myself, what exactly did he mean?

There was much else in our daily routine which he would have found familiar and of which he would have approved. Dr Reddie had impressed upon his boys that man was a trinity of hand, heart and brain, and had planned the timetable accordingly; the brain exercised every morning in class; the afternoons devoted to 'estate work' or manual labour and the evenings to social and cultural pursuits. This was our programme, too. The motto of the school was still 'Glad Day, Love and Duty', and the importance of service was still hammered home. Games were not allowed to become a fetish and we were given ample scope to pursue our own interests.

Father's first term at Abbotsholme, in the summer of 1897, had been, sadly enough, a miserable one. (He describes himself as a hopeless coward in the water and swimming instruction was rough and ready in those days. He was made to jump off the diving board into deep water.) Thirty-six years later, I was more fortunate and my first term was perhaps the happiest of my career. The weather, I am sure, had a lot to do with it. The summer of that year was the finest and hottest of the decade. Since we were encouraged to shed our clothing, sunburn was suddenly a problem. Tins of coconut oil were ordered and arrived in bulk and each boy was issued with his own greasy and leaky container. They accompanied us wherever we went and in consequence we all reeked of the South Seas and developed the most startling tans.

Our knickerbocker suits, worn at the beginning and end of term, were otherwise for use only on Sundays. We dressed in shorts and open-necked shirts during the week, a fashion followed by the Headmaster and all his staff. Since our masters were, on the whole, only slightly older than the senior boys – or so it seemed to me at first – it was often hard to tell which was which. We did not 'sir' them but commonly used their nicknames. There was little protocol, no fagging and no corporal punishment. The worst that could happen to you was to be sent for a run, and as each day in any case began with a run and a cold shower, this was not too much of a hardship.

At Parents' Gatherings and half-term weekends my father and mother would drive up from London to see me and stay for a couple of nights at the White Hart in Uttoxeter. Father had only recently become a driver and car owner, encouraged in the enterprise by an automotive development known as the 'fluid flywheel'. This mechanism, coupled with a pre-selection lever which enabled him to choose his gear in advance, removed any difficulty he might have experienced – he was not mechanically adroit – for when the right moment arrived he had only to press down a pedal. The first of our cars was a four-wheeled BSA. (This make was better known for its three-wheelers.) The humblest, the most modest of the range of vehicles equipped with the device, this was a typical first purchase, for my father was cautious in such matters, but by the time I was at boarding school he had promoted himself to Lanchesters. First we had the 10 and then the 12. On he went, growing bolder all the time, until the moment came, and it was a moment much savoured, when he bought his first Daimler, the royal car. True, ours was the baby Daimler, but his motoring ambitions were now satisfied and he was to keep with this model for the rest of his driving days.

37

Always, at these half-term weekends, we would lunch at a country inn, the Peveril of the Peak, or the Isaak Walton, where I would stuff myself enjoyably with hotel food. Sometimes, I would bring a friend along with me. I remember one particular boy – we must have been fifteen or sixteen at the time, approaching the top of the school – telling me after one of these outings, in tones of quite sharp envy, that he only wished he had a father like mine. I was a little taken aback, I think, for I was beginning to feel a certain ambivalence in my attitude towards him as a son, beginning to be aware, possibly, that I had a problem on my hands. Nevertheless, it was flattering and I felt a glow of pride. My friend had spoken with feeling; he was obviously sincere. And, of course, my father could make a brilliant first impression. He was, in his own way, extremely high-powered. He had only to extend himself and he could dazzle a stranger.

Let me end this chapter as I began it, with a letter received from him at school. This one is a light-hearted affair. For a change, he is in a thoroughly relaxed mood, holidaying in Iceland and far away from his business and publishing concerns.

'My dear old David,

I have got to the back of beyond. It took all day over rough and often precipitous tracks to get here in a 36 horse-power car, although it is rather less than 100 miles from Reykjavik. It is supposed to be a road, but you would not recognise it as such. Once here, the only means of transport is ponies. I was riding one for over 6 hours yesterday and the result is that today I am so sore that I don't want to sit down and so tired that I don't want to stand up ! ! There is a hot spring a few yards from the farmstead, so that one can go and have a hot tub out of doors. The spring provides central heating for the house – most convenient. The weather is changeable. This morning I was stretched at full length on the ground with my head on a tuft of grass without even a jacket on, tasting the joys of Feldeinsamkeit. In the afternoon I was not too warm with a coat or mack. (Feld=field. Einsam=alone or lonely.) There is a famous song by Brahms which Mummy used to sing called Feldeinsamkeit, in which the poet describes how he lay at full length in the sun in the tall grass and mused and dreamt.

The postal arrangements right out here are primitive. You first hand your letter to someone going to Ferncot (nearly 2 hours on pony back). He puts the letter in his pocket. *If* he remembers it he hands it to a farmer who is the local postal official (and much else). He puts it on his desk and says he doesn't think anyone will be going to Borganess today but there will probably be someone tomorrow. *If* there is he takes it in his pocket the 30 kilometres to Borganess; assuming that he does not return with it in his pocket he puts it on a derelict little steamer which does not sail every day and is expected to sink at any time! If the boat does not sink the letter will reach Reykjavik and then there would be some hope of your getting it. Now with all these stamps on it it might arouse so much curiosity that it would never reach you, so I am going to post it myself next Monday at the main post office in the capital.

Good luck to you at school. It will be jolly to see you again. Ever so much love old boy,
from your devoted Daddy,
Stanley Unwin.'

Seven

By now I have become an enthusiastic photographer and have bought a second-hand Rolleiflex for the unbelievably large sum of sixteen guineas. May I open my album and show you some of my prints? You will see that I am getting quite good results, but sadly enough for posterity (largely interested in people) I am 'artistic' and point my lens almost exclusively at trees, clouds and mountains. Figures appear infrequently and then usually in the middle distance, with their backs turned, to give scale. However, some of these land-scapes stir memories. Here is a view of Val d'Isère, for example; the scene of one of my father's few serious mistakes. Having studied a map, which gave the impression that the village was sited in a quiet cul-de-sac at the head of a high valley, he had booked us all in to the best hotel for our summer holiday. We arrived to find that, unbeknownst to him, a brand new trunk road had just been com-pleted, continuing on over the mountains and down into Italy. The main street was pandemonic with through traffic and, more up-setting still, the hotel, overwhelmed by an influx of visitors, had failed to reserve us our rooms. After a lot of trouble, inferior accommodation was found for us in a remote building. Father was confirmed in his feelings about the unpredictability and untrust-worthiness of the Latin races and we left in a day or two and spent the rest of our time in France at a big, peaceful, family hotel at Pralognan. And it was travelling home, on this occasion, that he had another memorable brush with the natives.

This took place at a large railway station where passengers, our-selves included, were herded behind bars, cooped up like horses at a starting gate, waiting for the barriers to open and permit us to board our train. When the moment came, it was arranged that I should speed ahead of the others and 'bag' an empty non-smoking compartment. This, being quick on my feet and unimpeded, I successfully did, and was standing in the doorway ready to repel all-comers when a French porter, larger and stronger than I was and laden with other people's luggage, thrust his way past me and began to heave suitcases into the racks. Father, who was following up the platform with our heavy luggage – as a family we *never* took porters – passed by outside the window and saw what was happening. The sight drove him berserk. I could hear him shouting in French and then he was upon us; sweeping aside resistance, grabbing the bags that had been inserted into the compartment and flinging them out into the corridor. How vividly I recall the triumphant *Whoops! Whoops!* accompanying each piece of luggage as it hurtled through the doorway. The porter retired, flattened, and we took possession. It was, indeed, a famous victory.

But to return to the photographs. Here, among the Swiss landscapes, is a family group which merits inspection. We are back in Lenzerheide again, it is the summer of 1935, and we are sitting under some fir trees at the edge of the lake. There is my brother Rayner, now a leggy nine-year-old, impish in shorts and sun hat, with mother beside him, composed, upright, neatly dressed. Ruth wears a bathing costume, as swimsuits were called in those days, and there is my father at the back of the group, contriving to look as alert and on the ball as ever, leaning forward in his open-necked shirt with a hand laid firmly upon the bare shoulder of a big and beautiful young woman; our cousin Peggy from New Zealand.

The gesture is an interesting one for, in spite of my mother's earlier comments, he was not often at ease in the company of the opposite sex. He was attracted, but he was fearful, too. Assured in business matters, he could be uncertain of himself – and his powers of resistance – when faced by a delightful woman. He found good-looking lady publishers and booksellers alarming to deal with because he automatically suspected them of employing their charms in order to get the better of him. But the grip of his hand on Peggy's shoulder is masterful and assured. How do we account for this? She is one of the family.

Short on pleasure, my father was strong on sublimation, which was fortunate because, as a man of principle, and hence morally hamstrung, there were things in his life which simply were not done. To be unfaithful to my mother was one of them. And as he possessed a warm physical nature, this may go some way to explain his dread of seductresses and to explain, too, why women outside the safe and secure circle of his relatives – and of his staff at the office – were so often and so erroneously classed as *femmes fatales*.

But here is another photograph which has somebody in it. The boy standing in the middle of the herd of goats is a schoolfriend from Abbotsholme. He is the same age as myself, sixteen; a precocious lad and already, he likes it to be known, a bit of a goat himself. He combines irresponsible bounce with pathetic helplessness and is always clamouring for people to do things for him which he should, by right, have been able to do for himself. Peggy is a favourite of his – she is born to be everyone's favourite – and he is under her spell. We two boys rag and tussle with her endlessly. We are like puppies; we will not leave her alone. She has an affectionate and pliable nature and a soft and pliable body and we take advantage of both. My favourite trick is to lock my arms round her waist and press my hands as hard as I can into the small of her back; whereupon she collapses weakly backwards and I find myself lying on top of her. How *could* she take our horseplay in such good part?

Turn over the page and we find still more prints of alpine scenery. But we are in Austria now, staying in Kitzbühel, and it is the summer of 1936. Here is a shot of the Kitzbühlerhorn taken from the terrace of the hotel. Father and I raced up to the summit and down again one morning before lunch. Since the climb itself was scheduled to take four hours and we had started after an eight o'clock breakfast, this was an indecently fast time and earned me a flattering glance from the hotelier's daughter – which, as I was still the son of my father in such matters, I failed to follow up. I think it serves to show, too, that my lungs must have made a satisfactory recovery.

There is, I am afraid to say, no record in my album of the trip Father and I made, that holiday, to Salzburg and Vienna, when I was present at the inception of perhaps the most dramatic of all his business *coups* : the rescue of the Phaidon Verlag, the Jewish firm of art book publishers, from the jaws of Hitler. I remember the office and the plump and unruffled figure of the owner, who seemed to be paying, I thought, insufficient attention to my parent's urgent pleas. If he wished to save his business, then he must act, and act quickly; but Dr Horovitz was not to be hurried and months went by and the suspense mounted. In the end, that interview turned out to be the first page of a riveting success story, a saga with a happy ending in which my father, waving his family tree, made himself the Aryan owner of a Jewish company, thus frustrating the wicked Nazis when they burst into Vienna. Good rousing stuff and all faithfully recorded in the book of his life. The climax might have been lifted from Buchan. 'When the time came for me to go, I accidentally ran into the Nazi lawyer in Berlin who had been handling Phaidon affairs. When he heard who I was he scowled and muttered, "You were too clever for us." ' Father adds a footnote : 'In September 1945 I learnt that I was in the Gestapo "Black List" of persons to be arrested immediately had the Germans invaded Britain.'

Another page to be turned. January 1937. Two young women and a young man are standing at the base of a metal cross studded with electric light bulbs. We are high above the river and vineyards, Kochem on the Mosel lies below us and we have been indulging in a little harmless target practice. Herbert, you will notice, is holding a pistol in his hand. His dark good looks are in marked contrast to his sister's fair prettiness. (I am already in love with Irmgard.) Anneliese is Herbert's girl-friend. I am a guest of the Neuer family and I am spending four of the happiest days of my life.

Herbert had completed his *Abitur* and was on short leave from his school, Schloss Bieberstein, which I had joined for the spring term. (Abbotsholme and the *Land-erziehungsheime*, the country boarding schools started by Kurt Hahn, the founder of Gordonstoun, had an exchange system : their boys came to us and we went to them.) We had made friends the previous year, which was why he had taken me home with him. And not very surprisingly after the bleak mountains of central Germany and the barren stone halls and corridors of the castle, perched in flamboyant style on an outcrop of rock and already suffering its first snowfalls of the winter, the balmy air of the sheltered river valley and the cosy ambience of the Neuers' house undermined any resistance I might have offered to blue eyes and golden curls. Herbert was about to become an officer in the army; Irmgard was a member of the Bund Deutsches Mädchen, and inevitably they were to be drawn into the war, Herbert dying in the Crimea, his sister ordered up to Rostock on the Baltic to work in a factory. But as far as we were concerned the war might never come, and so we thoughtlessly climbed the hills, visited the wine cellars, danced cheek to cheek to the sentimental *Tausend Roten Rosen Blühen* or the livelier *Wenn ich die Blonde Inge, Abends nach Hause bringe*. Wandering along the promenade beside the river, Irmgard and I stayed out so late one evening that Herbert was sent to fetch us back; which he did by firing his pistol repeatedly and shattering the small town's evening calm. And then, all too soon, came the time for our departure. I remember Frau Neuer's meaningful glance at me as we piled into the taxi. *'Ein schöner Zeit vorbei!'* Irmgard's loving gaze was fixed, to my regret, upon her brother, but we corresponded until the outbreak of war and again afterwards. I received my first news of her – and of Herbert's death – through the Red Cross.

We returned to Bieberstein to find the school shattered by an epidemic. More than half the boys were ill with a type of flu or tonsilitis. Work had stopped and the authorities had tried to get in touch with us in Kochem, to inform us that we could stay where we were; we had no need to return. If the news had reached us, the course of my life might have been drastically altered. So often it is through small chances and accidents like this that our steps are directed. And should any of my readers jump to a too hasty conclusion, I am not thinking about Irmgard. Our romance might have flowered, I suppose, but the timing was against it. No, I am returning once again to the subject of my health.

I was, of course, a sucker for germs. They leapt at me and within a few days I was laid low. But while my fellow-sufferers came and went, spending a few days in bed in the vast, vaulted hall which was the school sick room, I became a permanent fixture. The weeks went by and there I remained, a puzzle to nurses and doctors. At the end of the term, as I had still not recovered, my father flew out to Germany and brought me home, for I was in too weak a state to accomplish the journey alone. Back in London, I was medically examined and to everyone's consternation it was discovered that all was not well within. I had developed a murmur in my heart.

This, of course, was a basic reverse, but it was to prove, ironically, an ally rather than an enemy. In the circumstances of the late thirties, it may well have led to a considerable extension of my life.

Eight

To succeed in the business world, you must start on the bottom rung of the ladder. This was one of my father's favourite axioms, dear to his heart. What was the point, he used to ask me, of wasting three or four years at a university, acquiring a degree? Where did it get you? A bottom rung had done wonders for him. Why should he doubt that it would suit me, too?

We had discussed my future together on many occasions and he had always given me to understand that I was free to choose. I was expected to make up my own mind about whether or not I wished to enter the firm. There, of course, *was* the business, waiting for me, and a very good business, too. Sooner or later – well, he had no intention of retiring in the forseeable future – so, later perhaps than sooner, a prosperous publishing company would fall into my lap. Most young men would give their right hand for a chance like that. Graduates from universitites, all with excellent degrees, were hammering fruitlessly on the doors of the better-known publishing houses, begging for jobs. I was in the most extraordinary position and he hoped I was aware of it. On the other hand, he was certainly not going to stand in my way if . . . All the time he knew as well as I knew that my mind was a blank on the subject. I had no ideas whatever about what I wanted to do.

I was a callow eighteen-year-old; a sheltered fledgling still peeping over the edge of the nest. The world outside looked to me complicated and excessively demanding and I had grave misgivings about making good. (I think my instincts already old me that running a business was not my thing.) Thanks to my stop-and-go schooling, my chances of obtaining a place at a university were virtually nil. Edinburgh was mooted at one point, but my mother, perhaps recoiling on my behalf from the cold north, felt the place was much too far away. No, my role as elder son demanded that I hop, without delay, on to a lowly perch in George Allen & Unwin. This was what my father had always planned.

I had not gone back for my final term at Abbotsholme. My tonsils, which the doctors had decided were the cause of my troubles, had been extracted and I spent the summer recuperating at home. After a placid few months my heart calmed down and ceased to mutter and grumble. I was pronounced fit again and one morning in the early autumn of 1937, clad in a brand-new suit from the Fifty Shilling Tailors, I was launched into my publishing career.

My job was already settled: I was to be office boy. This minion, according to my father, shared an inestimable advantage with no less a person than the Chairman of the company. These two, although distanced from each other by the length of the ladder, were the only members of the firm who went everywhere and saw everything and were consequently in a position to view the business as a whole. (I think this supposes a certain degree of curiosity on the part of the lad who fetched, carried and ran the errands, and a degree of relaxation about the time allowed him to pursue his enquiries.) So, bracing myself for the responsibilities ahead of me, I arrived on my first morning and was taken aback to find I was in partnership, for there already was – as I might have guessed there would be – a perfectly good office boy working at the firm. And as his assistant and junior dogsbody, my foot seemed to have slipped from the important bottom rung. I had not even achieved *that* slight degree of elevation. I was left standing on the floor.

The building was Dickensian in quality; shabby and dusty and musty; a tangle of staircases linking poky rooms where gnomic figures lurked, bent over typescripts or ledgers. Ancient gas fires sputtered and, as the fogs descended, lights burned above the desks all day. Like an obedient retriever at his master's heels, I followed my colleague Peter through the labyrinth, delivering and collecting letters, linking department with department, and as the evening approached we were drawn more and more frequently through the heavily-sprung door and down the steep little flight of stairs that pitched into the Chairman's office. For not only was my father reading through and signing his own considerable output of letters; he was inspecting every letter that was sent out by the firm that day.

His office, like the rooms at home, barely changed while he was alive. The two shades of green on the walls; the green linoleum on the floor; the elongated sepia panoramas of the Southern Alps of New Zealand and the mountains above Lenzerheide, framed in black passe-partout and hanging each side of the fireplace; the Martin pots and the photograph of his mother above his desk, the surface of which was always covered with neatly-stacked heaps of papers; the heavy upright telephone quivering at the end of its lattice extension; all this has already been vividly described by my cousin Philip Unwin in his book documenting my father's – and his step-uncle Fisher Unwin's – publishing activities.* There is no need for me to dwell further on it, here.

I had quickly made friends with my office-boy partner, a cheerful cockney of Italian extraction and, as boys will, we fooled about together whenever we were given the chance. We soon ran into trouble and, as usual, I was to blame. Peter would have behaved responsibly if I had not been around all the time to set him a bad example. The hub of our activities, the front office, was shared by two quiet and respectable clerks. One of them occupied a desk at the back of the shop, out of harm's way, but the other, who spent his days painstakingly writing out invoices in his neat longhand, sat between the counter and the window. By virtue of his position, Mr Ryan was very much in the firing line.

I had discovered that I could leap, feet together, in one bound from the floor to the counter and stand there, balanced and proudly upright. This was my party trick and I was very pleased with it, but it had a disastrous effect upon my friend. For try as he might, and he did try frequently, he could not match this feat. I had the edge on him and he could not understand why. Always the slippery soles of his black leather shoes refused to grip and with waving arms he would totter and crash back to the floor. In the end he tried once too often and, tumbling wildly backwards, hit and shattered one of

* Philip Unwin, *The Publishing Unwins*; Heinemann, 1972.

the legs of Mr Ryan's chair. These athletic contests took place in the lunch hour, when we had the shop to ourselves, but the smashed chair took a great deal of explaining when our senior invoice clerk returned for his afternoon's work.

The office boy's job at Ruskin House was no sinecure. I was on my feet most of the day, running endlessly up and down the stairs or going out on errands, a break in the routine which I naturally enjoyed. Extra-curricular activities, such as jumping on to counters, were exertions my body could perhaps have done without. Whatever the cause, my symptoms returned; my heart began to bother me again; the doctors shook their heads and, before it had really got started, my stint at the foot of the publishing ladder had come to an untimely end.

Sitting at home with nothing to do, staring out into a garden barely visible through a curtain of yellow fog, I gloomed hopelessly on my lot. How unfair it seemed. I knew that within my invalid's carcase (like the thin man in the fat man) a lively, normal youngster was struggling to get out. But the moment he emerged and tried to enjoy himself, *slap*, he was knocked back. If my short life had a nadir, this was it.

My mother was not surprised. Father had jumped the gun as usual and, in his over-eager way, had involved me in much too much activity, too soon. With my track record, to start me off as office boy had been nothing short of lunacy. She was now in a splendid position to say, 'I told you so'. Why, if I *must* be put to work, had I not been settled quietly behind a desk? I was her delicate child, her cracked pot ('which always last the longest,' she was quick to add) and it must have been a relief when I was returned into her hands again. My ill-health had become a way of life for her, and now the pattern established so long ago in Lenzerheide, when my mother and I had effectively ganged up on my father, was about to be repeated. I was entering a period that would last for many years when, according to the vagaries of my unfortunate physique, I came under the domination of one or other of my parents.

Father was disappointed but he took it philosophically. He was

49

ready to agree that he had 'rushed me' and was now prepared to wait. He had high hopes of me, still, in spite of all these setbacks. One day, far ahead, when he was unable to carry it further, I would grasp the torch from his hand and bear it onwards. He looked forward to this. (The trouble was, while there was plenty of mileage in *his* legs, I did not seem to be able to stagger fifty yards.) His nature being Sagittarian and optimistic, he did not doubt that I would recover. '. . . a sun will pierce/The thickest cloud earth ever stretched.' Browning was his favourite poet.

As it happened, he was right. The sun *did* pierce the fog, lifting my spirits and restoring my body. Wrapped in the voluminous folds of a camel hair overcoat (it had cost eight pounds and was by far the most expensive article of clothing I had ever possessed) I would soon be heading south again with my family, to spend yet another therapeutic winter in the Alps.

Nine

We had this in common, my mother and I. We shared the joy, the sense of escape, in dodging out from under the drab blanket of the English winter sky. 'We are nearly blown away up here with March winds,' she writes from Hampstead in the spring of 1913, 'and today it's raining as well. Oh! I sometimes almost *die* with longing for the sun!' Unlike us, my father was rarely affected by the weather. He was much too busy and, holidays apart, only kept an eye on it on weekend afternoons.

January 1938, my first month at Lenzerheide I spend reclining in a deck chair with a rug over my knees. Mother sits beside me wearing a black fur hat. I compared myself in the last chapter with a fledgling peeping anxiously over the edge of the nest. I have now clearly tumbled out of it; but all is well, for mother bird is looking after me. A photograph taken at this time reveals all. I am lying back with an abashed, deprecating smile, as if apologising for being such a nuisance, while my parent, bolt upright, faces the camera with a possessive stare. Her expression leaves no doubt in the mind. *She* is in charge here.

Rest, mountain air and sunshine worked its usual magic and I was soon able to leave my chair and go for short walks along the snowy tracks. All about me were skaters and skiers indulging in strenuous physical activity and, viewing their unrestrained antics from the sidelines, I thought them almost wantonly irresponsible. In my enfeebled state, it seemed too much to hope that they would get away with it. My father had long ago returned to the office; Ruth and Rayner had gone back to their schools and even my mother eventually left my side. I was not deserted, however. Uncle Bernard, no longer teaching at Abbotsholme, was despatched to

51

keep me company. Poor chap, he arrived on the scenes too late and found himself involved in that most awkward social situation : two's company, three's none. I had fallen in love again, and again with a blonde.

She was as much a child of the place as I was, for her father had been a member of those early Lenzerheide parties in the days before the First World War. (There was, in fact, a closer link still between Harold Curwen, the printer, and Stanley Unwin, the publisher, for both had been to Abbotsholme.) Isobel was the offspring of Harold's first marriage. Her mother had died soon after she was born and her father was now married, but not happily, to his second wife, Freda. My parents, at an earlier stage, had been much involved with the Curwens, in particular with Isobel's mother, but the friendship had lapsed. I was to be instrumental in putting them in touch again.

When I first encountered her – she, too, was staying at the Lenzerhorn. Where else, indeed? It was and always had been 'our' hotel – she was flanked by two girl friends, one short, one tall. All three girls would sweep grandly into dinner wearing the backless, or at least back-plunging, evening dresses typical of the late thirties. I found the trio daunting and unapproachable. Although I yearned for a girl-friend, I entirely lacked the confidence to go out and get one. This last illness had in some measure detached me from my generation and turned me into a shy recluse. In the end, her body-guards returned to England. Somehow, I contrived to make an opening and spoke to her alone.

She dazzled me. I thought her spectacular. Studying the photographs I took of her that winter, I see that she was an attractive girl with a pleasant, open face : not by any means a classic beauty but with one arresting feature – her bell of smooth, straight and very bright fair hair, which flashed and glittered in the sun. But then the mountain sun was an alchemist, burnishing cheeks and forehead, gilding the skin, so that each day her smile seemed whiter, her blue eyes a more melting blue. My deck-chair was set on the ice-rink's edge and, lying there, I would see her skating towards me out of the morning sun, her long shadow reaching me before she did, her head aureoled, her hair a tissue of pale gold against the deep and thrilling colour of the sky. She was enchantment; she was liberation; she hoisted me out of the fogs of invalidism and depression into a heady empyrean where joy ruled and the senses sang hosannahs. A year ago, I realised, my feelings for Irmgard had been tentative, hesitant. *This* was the real thing.

Like me, she had no sense of vocation, no strong feelings about what she wanted to do. We had this in common. We differed, in that she was financially independent. She was free. She had no job at that time but, since she had her own income, she could afford to stay on in Lenzerheide for as long as she wanted. To my delight, she postponed her departure and the idyll continued. She did not – could hardly be expected to – return my ardour. She was calmer, more level-headed (it would be difficult to find anyone more extravagantly tilt-headed than I was at that stage) and was also a few years older. She bore with my torrent of talk and found me, I think, sufficiently diverting. The situation was new to her. She had not had a young man prostrate himself at her feet – or skating boots – before.

My uncle, meanwhile, was keeping a low profile. Put in an anomalous position, how well he reacted. But then he was a sweet person; gentle and sensitive and understanding. We were with him every evening and he often joined us for lunch at one or other of our peaceful mountain retreats. I may have missed out on university, but my education was proceeding none the less, for I was beginning to get to know, and to understand slightly, men who differed in every way from my father. This was salutary, for I had to some extent been brainwashed – my own fault, due to slow development, faulty equipment or both – and I had anticipated an adult (male) world peopled almost exclusively with replicas of Stanley Unwin. I was astonished and much relieved to find that this was not in the least the case : to discover, in fact, that *he* was the odd man out; a singular exception to the general rule.

Short, stocky, with thick greying locks and a square, strong craftsman's face, my uncle was a handsome man. He, too, had tales to tell, but they rang a little differently to the tales I was wont to hear. He had been in America, he told me, where he had met and

53

fallen in love with a girl and she with him. She proved to be an heiress, a millionaire's daughter. This was daunting for he was impecunious, but the girl's father had taken him on one side and told him not to worry; he had enough money for both of them. In spite of this, Bernard had not married her. Was he too proud, perhaps? Too independent? He never explained, but I thought it a great pity.

I knew that in his youth he had behaved strangely at times, but some of his actions were very far from mad. It was his misfortune to be a visual man brought up among ugly objects. He had once run through the rooms of the family house, smashing the pictures with a hammer. And *this* was produced as proof that he was insane! How I felt for him, having been brought up myself with far too many of those gloomy, dark brown reproductions in their stained oak frames.

I knew, too, that he had inherited to an almost morbid degree the Unwin bump of conscientiousness. (His was a more intense and irrational version of the bump that afflicted Father.) He was walking one day with a party of friends in a country of stone walls – the Dales, perhaps, or the Lake District. Returning late from their excursion, darkness and rain overtook them and they left the path and ran straight down the hillside, clambering over various walls on the way. In their hurry, they dislodged a few stones from one of them, but did not stop to do anything about it. The weather was bad; they were tired; they were eager to get back to the hotel. This worried Bernard. He brooded about those tumbled stones through the evening meal and carried the guilt of them to bed, where he tossed and turned restlessly. In the end he got up again, dressed and, taking a torch, let himself out into the night. Only after he had climbed the steep hillside and repaired the wall would his conscience permit him to sleep.

The month of March arrived, and with it came a change of guard. My uncle was due to return home and Isobel, to my sorrow, had also decided she must leave. Her father had not been well and, thinking the change might do him good, she arranged that he should come out and stay with me. I found the prospect slightly daunting. He was a stranger, although he had known me as a child, and I was uncertain what to expect. I need not have worried. We were at ease with each other almost at once.

Harold Curwen was a diffident man and a quiet speaker, who spilled his ideas out slowly but with nice flashes of humour; a gentle man who made not the smallest attempt to bounce, browbeat or convert. We had photography in common and when, not long after his arrival in Lenzerheide, we decided to go down together to the Tessine, we found subjects in plenty for our lenses. Spring came early in 1938; camelias, magnolias were in flower; the chestnut buds were breaking on the promenade at Lugano; there were puffs of pink almond blossom on the hillsides above the azure lake. This was my first glimpse of the south, of a romantic, Italianate landscape, and I found it the country of my dreams.

We took rooms in a pension, where we breakfasted every morning in hot sunshine on our balcony. Steamers criss-crossed the lake, linking village with village, and as the flawless days went by we explored them all. Some were perched dramatically over the water, campaniles and slender cypress spires punctuating the skyline; others, low and sprawling, extended themselves along their waterfronts, the crumbling, colour-washed façades of their old buildings mirrored in the still surface. Everything we saw pleased us, for everything was harmonious and satisfying : the vaulted stone roofs of the arcaded streets; the graceful shapes of the coracles with their hooped canopy frames. Nothing ugly marred the scene. No cement apartment blocks had yet arrived to make nonsense of the scale, and no pylons or electricity poles yet disfigured the wooded hills.

We lingered contentedly there for a week or two; then, sending our luggage on in advance and carrying rucksacks, we set off to walk by slow stages up to Airolo, where the great mountain wall lifts and blocks away the north. For the moment had come when I must turn my back on all things lovely and stiffen myself to face the cold douche of reality that I knew must be awaiting me in England. A very wonderful winter was, at long last, coming to an end.

Ten

Father was waiting to meet us on the Continental arrival platform at Victoria station. We had both rather hoped that he would not put himself to the trouble : but there he was.

When I glimpsed him from the carriage window, a smallish figure in a neatly buttoned overcoat, his beard neatly clipped, hands clasped in front of him; so spruce, so organised, so together; stream-lined, in the sense that a high-explosive shell is streamlined (latent force ready to burst from a trim, restrained exterior), his gaze so sharp, so direct, so artless, and I saw my big, disorganised, far from together, hopelessly complicated companion flinch, look hunted and withdraw defensively within himself; then, for the first time in my life, I became aware of the devastating effect my parent could have on other people. You had to be a bold confident spirit – or a fairly simple one – thoroughly to appreciate his qualities. You met his challenge, you viewed him uncritically, or you went under. I was concerned to find Harold Curwen was doing just that.

I already knew, for we had talked openly on our travels, that he found my father a difficult and overpowering man, someone he was unable to stand up to, whom he dreaded to meet. As the boat train rattled through the Kent countryside I had watched him grow appreciably more nervous. I was feeling a little uneasy, too. I was now a friend of Harold's and to that degree had distanced myself and had taken a first decisive step away. I knew in my heart that I had gone over. I was now on the other side. Clearly, though, Harold found the prospect of being met by him far more daunting than I did.

And my father? Had he the ghost, the glimmer of an idea of what might be passing through our minds as the train steamed in?

I think not. He was too confident, too full of the pleasure of being himself, too involved with his own personality to relate effectively to other people. He was a parent meeting his elder invalid son, now recovered and about to settle down to work again. He was a commercially-successful and highly-regarded publisher meeting an old school friend, a talented printer, who had made quite a name for himself although, in business terms, he must rate as a comparative failure. He saw everything in simple, bold, clear outlines. He was in no sense subtle and had no time – or understanding – for hints and nuances. He had taken an hour off from the office to meet us, not only because he would have felt it his duty to do so, but because he loved me. He may have had his limitations but he was a well-intentioned man.

Soon after my return we had a long and serious talk together, sitting under the pear tree in the strip of the Old Garden not already occupied by the tennis court. And we could not tune into one another's wavelengths. We were at loggerheads.

Thirty years earlier, when as a young man he had taken an un-precedented two-month break in Europe, he had felt much as I did. In his journal of that time he tells us that 'every now and then one is overcome with a strange happiness, a feeling that it is good to be alive. With me it always comes out in the open, when I have been able to throw off all thought of business, and this morning when I was in that happy state I longed to bring out here some of the blasé, worn-out youths of London, not so fortunate as myself, and ask them, "Doesn't this make life worth living?" ' Sadly enough, these feelings had long been overlaid and forgotten and I was confronted with a sober man of affairs, practical and down to earth in his attitudes and entirely out of sympathy with my restless yearnings.

I found him shuttered and dead to everything that mattered to me; unmoved, while I desperately tried to defend and protect those values I had – not perhaps discovered – but recently re-affirmed. Beauty was truth, truth beauty at that moment, for I had come back to Hampstead drenched in colour and light; imbued with the spirit that moves through all things; in essence a mini-Wordsworth

57

with a dash of Keats and Richard Jefferies to spice the mixture, and physically lit up in to the bargain. Haltingly, I tried to explain myself, and he listened with mounting impatience. What had all this to do with earning a living? he asked me. How would the world go round if all young people took my attitude? I had had a long length of rope; over-long, he feared, for my own good. The sooner I buckled down and started my life in earnest, the better. I must not forget that I had my way to make. No one would do it for me.

I see now that this was a key moment. If I had boasted a modicum of talent or guts, I would have swung a guitar or an easel across my back and stumped off into Europe to try my luck. But a move as bold, as rebellious as this was, of course, beyond me. The idea was unthinkable, not just because I was incapable of painting a picture or playing an instrument – there were other ways of scraping along – but because I had been over-protected all my life and had not yet stood for two minutes together on my own feet. My health had had something to do with this, but not all. It is hard, today, to convey a true impression of the claustrophobic quality of middle-class family life in the thirties. The young would-be rebel might sulk and grumble privately, but he usually ended by doing what he was told to do. I am sorry to say that I was no exception to this depressing rule.

I was not, however, sent back to the office. All were agreed that the bottom rung would have to wait. I think the débâcle of the previous autumn had had its effect on my father and I am certain that my mother would not have permitted a second attempt. Those who did not know my parents were apt to underestimate her power over him; they assumed, on the evidence presented, that he dominated her life. This, to an extent, he did, but she was capable of influencing him when she was sufficiently roused to make the effort, and she was a tireless behind-the-scenes champion of her children's rights. They had a dialogue, my parents, although it might not be immediately apparent to those around them. I would say they talked mainly in bed.

Thwarted in his attempt to place me on the ladder, Father adjusted his sights. Before I took my place in Museum Street, he now determined, I must be trained. It was vital to my ultimate success that I make myself familiar with the ancillary industries : I must master the techniques of printing, paper-making, book-binding and the like, after which I could turn my attention to the book trade proper. A stint of work at a good bookseller might follow and then a spell as traveller 'on the road'. In theory, this was all excellent but in practice my father's shots often misfired or hit unexpected targets. He opened the programme with a sighting shot so wildly tangential, so divorced from London book publishing reality, that I feel sure my mother must have grabbed at the barrel of the gun. I was to be sent out to Geneva, to work in the Publications Department of the League of Nations.

There were, in fact, various quite good reasons why this move suited, but none of them had much bearing on my future. Father, it was clear, had had to compromise and my mother's logic had won the day. Switzerland, it was now established, was good for my health and my sister was already in Geneva. She was settled happily into a pension in Petit Saconnex, studying French. Watching over her in the role of a guardian figure was a close friend of my father's, Fritz Schnabel, who was the Director of the department in question. And as Allen & Unwin were the agents for League publications in Great Britain, there was a link of a sort between Ruskin House and the secretariat.

Fritz had been a childhood hero of mine, a much-adored figure, and from my earliest days I had occupied a warm corner in his affections. He was an attractive, ebullient man with a big broad face, kindling eyes and an infectious smile. His hair was no longer thick but curled nicely at the back of his neck. He had begun life as an actor, which perhaps explained his larger-than-life projection of himself and his charisma. We had not seen each other for a number of years.

To judge by photographs taken at the time, I must have been a pleasing, eager little boy. I was now a gauche and spotty youth. Fritz could not quite conceal his disappointment. And to confound me further, my eighteen-year-old sister had stepped into my shoes. She had become the undisputed queen of his affections : I was nowhere. This was a strange and rather galling sensation. Always in the past I had considered Fritz to be *my* friend.

They met me at the airport in Fritz's car, which had two seats under the hood in front and a folding dickey behind. This, naturally, was where I sat; then and on the various excursions we made that summer up into the Jura mountains. Perched there, blown about in the open air, I could dimly discern through the semi-opaque mica window the backs of the others' heads, although I was unable to hear what they were saying. I remember that dickey seat with dislike, for it served to underline my isolation. (Absurdly shy, I could not even bring myself to bang on the window to signal I needed to relieve myself. I preferred to sit and suffer.) There were always three of us because Irma, Fritz's wife, never joined the party; which meant, to my discomfiture, that it had now become my turn to play Uncle Bernard's role of gooseberry. If I had felt a little less piqued, I might have been more understanding.

The perks and privileges – yes, and a large share of the devotion – had come my way, not hers, while we were growing up. It is true to say that I had been treated as a first-, my sister as a second-class citizen in our home. (My parents were oddly neglectful in this respect.) Now, for the first time, she was being given something she needed. 'What a field of warmth and continental charm I encountered,' she was to write many years later. 'My view of life was broadened and I learned so much. I shall always remember my time in Geneva for a feeling of being loved and a new awareness of beauty.' She adds rather touchingly. 'It was wonderful to feel I mattered to someone. Part of me was so *glad* to be noticed.' This aspect of the relationship passed me by. Mine was a simple schoolboy's view : he likes her better now than he does me. If I had been more alert, I might have grasped that Fritz was playing an important and a necessary part in her development. Certainly, without him, her days would have been dull and circumscribed.

The atmosphere in that staid and stuffy villa in the Avenue de Mervelet was hardly a merry one. I was to live with Mlle Cosson-Dupan for almost a year and I grew very fond of her, but she was a formidable ancient, a disciplinarian who stood no nonsense and the ruler of the household, although Hélène, her devoted cook-general, did all the work. She took a lot of trouble over us and taught us French extremely well.

The villa was in a leafy suburb, a long tram ride from the centre of the city. Fritz had arranged for Ruth to be boarded here, for Mlle Cosson did not run a regular pension : apart from one trembling old lady with Parkinson's disease, we were the only paying guests. He and Irma lived a few streets away and he came round regularly for a French lesson one or two evenings a week. These visits were cheering events. He would breeze in, big and beaming, effervescent as always, and set us spinning like tops with the whip of his presence. Mlle Cosson dressed up for the occasion, Hélène would put on her best apron, and I would hear my sister singing like a happy bird – *Er der Herrlichster von allen* – for the hour before he was due to arrive.

My job at the League of Nations was not to start until September and I marked time in Geneva, that summer, waiting on the postman's knock. I had last glimpsed Isobel waving goodbye to me from the window of a yellow post bus in Lenzerheide. Before my return to England, she had crossed the Atlantic and was now staying with relatives in Florida. We wrote to each other every few days and I had mementoes with me, a woollen glove, an album of photographs, to keep my memory warm.

In spite of all this, my heartstrings were pulled taut by distance. I suffered, and Mlle Cosson viewed the peaks and troughs of my emotional life with dry detachment. Faced across the work table with sighs and languors and a regrettable lack of attention to the matter in hand, she would pull me up with a sharp, 'David ! *Tu es trop sentimental.*' My favourite writer was Lamartine; my most adored book, his *Graziella*. The Mediterranean ! Young sunburnt love ! I underlined the most shamelessly romantic passages and read them again and again.

Father was also in Europe that summer : first in Germany, at Leipzig and Berlin, for the Congress of the International Publishers Association – as retiring President he had no choice but to attend and hand over his gavel of office, but he saw to it that the Nazis were given no opportunity to use the platform for political or propaganda purposes – and then in Czechoslovakia on the invitation of a group of publishers. Success had now caught up with him, and he writes buoyantly to my mother on the night of his arrival in Prague.

> 'Dearest, I little thought when I quitted this beautiful town in the pouring rain as an almost penniless youth about 34 years ago that I should arrive on the next occasion by air, let alone be met by a deputation of 3 leading publishers and personally conducted by car from the airport to my hotel where a suite had been reserved for me! However, here I am!'

On his way home from these junketings he called in at Geneva to see us, and he must have made some instant arrangements on my behalf, for I can remember a strange and unsatisfactory sequence of jobs, dream-like in retrospect, for they bear so frail a link with reality; which, while they disturbed the pattern of my days, could not be said to have contributed much towards my publishing education.

Superbly confident and entirely unstoppable, he would set up these situations with the speed of light, sweeping me with him, a helpless victim, into whatever bookshop or printing works happened to have taken his fancy. His name was known all over Europe. A flourish of his visiting card and we instantly landed up in the Director's office, face to face with a polite, deeply-puzzled but respectfully-attentive gentleman behind a desk. The demand was made – it would be a most valuable experience and of great benefit to his son if he could be allowed to work here for a short time. Could a job be found for him, on a voluntary basis? – and they were met, not always enthusiastically, sometimes indeed very reluctantly, but my father was persuasive and he was never refused. What, however, was the net result? I would arrive on the following Monday morning to find, instead of a polite Director, one harassed departmental head after another, none of whom had the faintest idea what to do with a youthful and inexperienced Englishman with a halting command of the language and an obvious lack of any useful skills or capabilities. So I would be passed rapidly down the line, accents growing rougher, lounge suits giving way to overalls and dungarees, until some suitably safe and menial chore could be found for me. I remember packing up magazines at a long counter in one firm and cleaning thick, honey-coloured lithographic stones at another; a figure of impenetrable mystery to the labourers about me, who could not begin to comprehend what I was doing in their company.

These jobs apart, our humdrum life at Petit Saconnex revolved round meals – Hélène was an excellent cook – and our French lessons. I made an attempt to be sociable and joined the Maison d'Etudiants, an international students' club, but I found my contemporaries much too alarming to be good company. They seemed to have an edge on me in every conceivable way. I was immature and timid and did not fit in. Sadly enough, events are now going to show that I was a prig as well.

The three of us had set off from Geneva in Fritz's car one hot Saturday or Sunday afternoon in high summer and snaked our way up into the cooler heights of the Jura mountains. Here we stopped in a glade among the trees and, after a while, I wandered away from the others with my Rolleiflex. This was the normal pattern, for at that time I was spending happy hours with my face buried in the hood extension, composing my landscapes on the little ground glass screen. Perhaps, that day, the surroundings were not sufficiently photogenic; perhaps I was missing some item of equipment; whatever the reason, I made a brief circuit and then wandered back again. And I found, to my shocked surprise, Fritz and my sister lying on the grass together, happily clasped in one another's arms.

I was guileless; my amazement proves it. I had not sneaked up on them to 'catch them out'. Since my arrival I had ignored every warning signal; that there might be a physical side to their friendship had simply not occurred to me. What I saw in front of me was idyllic, innocent – but as far as I was concerned, inconceivable. He was a man of about my father's age; hale, vigorous, but a parent figure. I was not yet twenty and it was the age-gap beyond anything that I found upsetting.

Fritz was as disconcerted as I was. He could not hide his embarrassment; starting up in a hurry, thoroughly put about.

We glossed things over and repaired the afternoon as best we could, but I returned to Mlle Cosson's that evening with a weight upon my mind. Fritz had been put in charge of Ruth; she had been entrusted to his care. And as the man responsible for her welfare, it seemed to me that he was exceeding his duties. This sort of thing had no place in the itinerary. What might happen next? I was her brother and I shared the responsibility, yet I lacked the confidence and the know-how to deal with the matter on the spot. I felt I had to do *something*, however, so I wrote to my parents. This was my duty as I conceived it, they had to be informed, but I could have hardly done anything more destructive. My letter caused an explosion in Hampstead; shock waves battered us; life in Geneva was never to be the same again.

The oddest, the most topsy-turvy, of all the repercussions and certainly the one that left me most bewildered was my interview with Fritz's wife. In my naive, unworldly way I had looked to her as an ally; surely *she* was on my side? Summoned to the Schnabel house, I faced instead her indignation. She could not understand why I had acted in this way. Fritz, she tried to explain, was doing my sister no harm. On the contrary, he was helping her. Ruth was ready for this awakening, and who better to watch over and encourage her than a man of his age and experience? How passionately she tried to convince me; tall, rather solemn, child-like Irma. But she could not get through; there was a gulf between us. My conditioning was too strong and the ethos of my youthful and arrogantly-intolerant puritanism – physical love was only for the young in years – made it impossible for me to sympathise. 'It all seems so harmless, looking back,' my sister writes. 'With Fritz it was only holding hands and kissing. Irma knew I was in love with him and loved me tenderly in spite of it.'

Father had few friends. Fritz Schnabel was one of them and my revelation irreparably damaged their relationship. Mother never forgave him. In her eyes, his conduct was indefensible. She sent him a letter which I have heard described as 'blistering'. Father was not prepared to take up so extreme a position. As a person he was too responsible and trustworthy – quite apart from other barriers – to contemplate an equivalent action himself, but he could understand why Fritz had been tempted.

Ruth's stay in Geneva came to an end soon after. My parents, understandably, wanted her home. She did not blame me for my behaviour, which she took in remarkably good part, for she considered that it was justified and that I had acted for the best. I had cared about her and 'that was such a lovely feeling in itself'. Always more self-contained than I was, she did not open up and discuss the matter with the family until early in the following year. The event gave my father so much pleasure that he sent me a flying note :

'I feel I must just send you a line to let you know that Ruth has had frank talks first with Mummy and now with me. She is feeling ever so much happier in consequence and we have a great weight lifted off our minds. In fact I could almost dance with joy! It was sweet to hear her appreciative reference to you. She seems to have come through with flying colours and her character will be strengthened because of the experience. I hope and think it may help to make her more open and frank in future. Anyway we are a happy family once again. You have a quite remarkable sister.'

And he followed this up a week or two later with a more lengthy – and very reasonable – appraisal of the situation :

'I think the sooner the whole incident is now forgotten the better. You have done your part manfully and nothing more is called for. I should be sorry if it poisoned to the slightest extent either your or Irma's relationship with Fritz. There is no reason why you should let it affect you. It is much easier for *me* to understand some aspects of the affair than it is for Mummy and I try to remember those wise words "Judge not that ye be not judged." Despite any "armour of self-contentment" the knowledge that there had been gossip must have been frightfully humiliating and they must be relieved to be going to South America. Don't forget that Fritz is staying on in Geneva partly on your account and has put himself out to be of help to you. I should hate him to have any excuse for feeling that any of us were unmindful of, or ungrateful for, that.

You will understand that what is at the back of my mind is anxiety to be scrupulously fair to him. Hélène will agree with me if you tell her that I reminded you that "all things work together for good to them that serve the Lord".

Goodnight you dear old boy.'

I stayed on in Geneva until the following spring, working under Fritz, and on fine days we would walk down to the office together. But in spite of my father's hopes, regretfully, we were never really at our ease again.

Eleven

I am sitting on the polished wooden seat of a third-class Swiss railway carriage. Somewhere out there in the blackness beyond the window is the Lake of Geneva. My face is burnt brown and my body agreeably tired after a weekend in the mountains. I am on my way back to Petit Saconnex and I am reading an absolutely riveting novel : *Queer Street* by Edward Shanks.

The book is set in London, but this is a London I have never glimpsed nor, until now, even guessed existed. I knew that my parents, my relatives, would have found it equally strange. What is more, they would have disapproved most strongly. I knew they would have hated this world and found the behaviour of its denizens abhorrent. *I* found them in a funny way quite sympathetic. No wonder I was enjoying the book so much.

All these people belonged to exciting little clubs where they were constantly meeting each other and where they spent their time gambling and drinking and making love. Not a man, not a woman seemed to be engaged in anything as dull or prosaic as earning a living. This meant that they were often in debt, of course, and awkward things kept happening to them, but that made their lives eventful and stimulating and jolly to read about. Their gambling and love-making I found interesting up to a point but what glued my nose to the page was their drinking. These extraordinary people were constantly ordering and consuming drinks. Right on through the length of those twin Penguin volumes they were ceaselessly at it; hardly a paragraph but a drink was downed. (I was tempted to make a count of them for interests' sake, but the size of the task daunted me.) And they were so cheerful and unconcerned about it, taking all those whiskys and gins and cocktails completely as a matter of course. I was absorbed, as well I might be. In real life I had hardly met anyone who *drank*.

Father permitted no alcoholic liquor to enter our home. That was the rule, but had there been one startling exception? Could it be that once, when Uncle Jack was having a meal with us, a bottle of cider was acquired for his consumption and placed on the table in front of his plate? Unlikely as this seems, I believe I can remember the solid, satisfactory shape of the flagon, massively built, boldly assertive, dwarfing in its masculine way my father's slender, feminine bottle of Cydrax, cider's little sister. Even admitting this, it is true to say that drink played no part whatever in our lives. The subject was a closed book. I was by this time twenty years old, yet I would have found it as impossible, as unthinkable, to walk into a public house and order a drink for myself as to enter a brothel. (Seven years later, on my honeymoon, I was still not able to bring myself to go into the bar of the friendly small hotel where we were staying.)

Father and I were soon to clash over drink. Given our temperaments, a contest of some kind was inevitable. He was such an adamant man; so inflexible; so easily outraged. The habit, he felt, was pernicious. Alcohol was dangerous stuff, one drink always led to another, and before you knew where you were you were totally demoralised. A drunken person disgusted him to the depths of his being. He was unable to envisage safe territory between abstinence and excess : such an area, in his view, was cloud-cuckoo land. If you were wise – and he obviously hoped I would be wise – you never set foot in it. In many ways, my father was a fearful man.

Why did the idea of drink so appal him? He came from an abstemious family, but then so do I. This fact alone cannot explain his attitude. However, he was involved at an impressionable age in a particularly sordid incident which he constantly talked about and which he describes in detail in his autobiography. This might be part of the answer.

'A fashionable lady from Bromley drove up in a carriage and pair in a state of great excitement to announce that

68

her dressmaker, whom she had learnt Mother also employed, had locked herself up in her little room with several bottles of spirit and had not left the room for any purpose for three (it may have been four) days and nights; that she refused to open the door; was incoherent, and, as far as could be seen through the keyhole, was lying on the floor, and would Mother do something about it. Why she came to Mother instead of tackling the job herself she did not explain. After she left, Mother said she was going down to see what she could do. I refused to let her go alone and accompanied her. As all the hammering on the door had no effect, I decided that we must try bluff, and yelled "Fire". There was a slight stir, a figure dragged itself along the floor and turned the key. I have seen some filthy pigsties in my day, but they were pleasant compared with the sight that met our eyes! There on the floor in the midst of the mess was a black and indescribably dirty mass of humanity, sodden with urine and worse. The stench was revolting. After one glance Mother observed calmly, "We cannot expect the other people here to deal with this; we must take her home". I could only gasp. "You had better get a cab", she said. The struggle to get that huge sodden mass down the stairs (she was a big woman) is one I will never forget.'

Poor Father; this was only a foretaste. All his life he was to be pursued by drunks. Loathing and detesting them, it was uncanny how often he seemed to attract them to his vicinity. They would appear in the most unexpected quarters and on the most embarrassing occasions. Whenever I was in his company I was always half on my guard, knowing that at any moment some drunk could turn up to annoy him. A typical encounter took place at an election night dinner at his Pall Mall club, a hallowed and dignified institution where decorum is the rule, voices are seldom raised and an obstreperous and inebriated member is as much a *rara avis* as a Dodo or a Great Auk. Needless to say he arrived on the scene *that* night and – the dining-room is a large one – at the adjacent table. We had a quiet and respectable Swedish Senator with us and, like a conscientious parent dealing with a child in a high chair, our guest spent much of his time darting across to rescue toppling and flying pieces of equipment. But even he could not keep order. Things grew rowdier and less manageable and there was a splendid climax when the cloth and the entire contents of the table were deposited in a heap upon the floor. I found the experience not without interest (this, after all, was the kind of behaviour you usually saw only in films) but my father was revolted. He informed me later, with much satisfaction, that the member had since been black-balled.

However, he did not allow prejudice to over-rule his common sense. This is revealed by a yellowing newspaper cutting which he must have sent to my mother before they were married. Above the headline: 'FLOGGING ADVISED FOR DRUNKARDS. Bold Suggestion by a London Doctor', he had written 'ROT! You might as well flog for measles.'

As a young man, I was certainly not bold, but my nature was empirical, and to block out an entire area of experience I felt was rather a pity. Some years before, as a schoolboy, I had drunk a glass of rather strong wine in France, pressed on me by an hospitable landlady, and I had had to grip the edge of the table to hold myself in place. That, and a half-pint or two of draught cider on school 'hikes' was, to date, all I had to work on. Spirits were as far removed from my world as dangerous drugs. No wonder I was drawn to Queer Street! No backsliding monk could have extracted keener excitement from a dose of soft porn than I from those heady scenes of gulping and quaffing. The sexual act, I knew, must wait for marriage – this was the creed of my upbringing; an edict against which I never attempted to rebel – but the thrills of drink lay just over the horizon. And so the train roared on towards Geneva and the Petits Suisse, biscuits and glass of milk laid out for me by the faithful Hélène when I returned late on a Sunday evening, and the book continued to joggle happily in my hand.

*

Five days a week I might be working at the League, but I lived for those weekends and my solitary excursions into the mountains. Nature, I had discovered, was the Great Healer and, thanks to her aid, I was rapidly and effectively mending a broken heart.

Isobel had returned to England at the end of July and my parents had invited her to join us in the Bernese Oberland, where we were renting a châlet for our family summer holidays. She had written me a brief, rather cold note from London, very different in tone from the warm and friendly epistles from the States. What had happened? Why had she changed? I met her at the station at Grindlewald and knew at once from her face, her greeting, that it was all over. She had met another man on the boat crossing the Atlantic and she was in love with him. He was a philosopher, no less; older, mature, undoubtedly a more suitable partner for her in every way. I wept. I was done for. I had never been so unhappy in my life before.

She stayed with us for a fortnight and after a day or two I cheered up and we swung into step together as companions, went on long walks and bathed in icy mountain streams. We must have given a strong impression of youthful and not unattractive camaraderie, for a total stranger stopped us and insisted upon taking our photograph. And as soon as she had gone I went for comfort and to unburden myself, as I always did in moments of distress, to my father and mother.

I must have approached them in the evening, at a late hour, for they were already in bed. Their room contained two bulky single beds, mounded with white Swiss 'puddings' or duvets, and these were set foot against foot along the length of the far wall, so that my parents, propped on their pillows, sat facing each other but at a considerable distance. My mother's face glistened with its nightly coat of cold cream. I told them my sad story and was instantly, as I knew I would be, enveloped in parental love, loyalty and concern. But, of course, there was nothing they – or anyone else – could do, and when the holiday was over and the family returned to England, I took my heartbreak back with me to Geneva. A letter from my father reached me soon afterwards.

'You have certainly had a bit of a cold douche but it has confirmed my confidence in you that you have treated it philosophically and extracted wisdom from what must obviously have been a shock. It is a great satisfaction that you have found *yourself* again because you have thereby regained your independence and enhanced your self control – factors of which I am afraid I never cease to urge the importance. But this is not a sermon – merely an occasion to say "well done, old boy". These troubles have an amazing way of working out for the best and anyway are invaluable experience.'

His relief, later that autumn, when I was able to write home cheerfully again was expressed in another and most revealing letter; one in which he lays down for my instruction what can only be described as a battle strategy. That I was, by temperament and inclination, wholly unsuited to take advantage of any such plan of action had not, apparently, occurred to him. The very idea of a war of the sexes was alien to my nature, and has remained so.

'When I read your letter this morning I could have almost cried for joy that I had such a wise son because, as the Chinese proverb says, "a wise man adapts himself to circumstances as water shapes itself to the vessel that contains it."

It is so wonderful that you fully realise that neither Mummy nor I want to decide things for you or curb your precious individuality in the slightest. As you know, we were more than ready to believe that Isobel might be the one intended for you and welcomed her accordingly. The recent episode was providential in that it revealed in good time something fundamental which made it clear that lasting happiness was unlikely along that road. Her own attitude I can well understand. She enjoyed your devotion and her sense of power over you. No girl likes to give up power over a man.

At a distance your mind is made up but at close quarters – particularly if there were any physical contact –

you might find it all very difficult. Dancing with her for instance would soon re-stimulate your physical feelings and the physical side can be the very devil.

However, you know all this and there is no need to labour it. Personally I see not the slightest reason for regret about the whole affair. You had a wonderfully romantic and enjoyable time – you have nothing of which to be ashamed – you have gained an invaluable experience which will serve you and possibly even save you later on. You are o'er young to be thinking about matrimony. Your career should I think come first. But by all means make fresh contacts. Remember that it is seldom wise to make any girl feel you are "easy prey." Your instinct – I refer to your deluging girls with letters – is apt to lead you astray. You behave as if you had hooked your fish. It is all right when you have done so (and are formally engaged) but, in the process of catching, the fly has continually to be withdrawn!'

Meanwhile, Munich was upon us and another of his letters reflects the tensions of the time. He gives a typically succinct political résumé of events; for he was, as usual, following every move with the keenest possible attention.

'Every day throughout this appalling crisis I have been saying "Thank God David is in Geneva and Rayner is at Abbotsholme." * Much as Mummy and I would love to have you with us, it is a great relief to feel you are out of London.

I do not believe that even Adolph Hitler knows what he has in store for us (and himself). He seems to be in an incredibly emotional if not hysterical state. That the whole world should find itself dependent upon the whims of such a man is an unbelievable situation.

Poor old Chamberlain! What a hell of a time he is having and what a responsibility! Whatever one may feel about his policy he has meant well and has undoubtedly

* A wry note from my sister. 'Where's Ruth? In London!'

done his best. Parliament is now assembling and I wait their deliberations with great interest.

It seems to me that friend Mussolini is now becoming a bit anxious; it is just conceivable that *he* may do something to hold Hitler back at the last second. The trouble is that the Germans do not yet believe or realise that we mean business . . . *if* we do, because our action depends upon a somewhat fickle France. Appeals from America to Hitler are uselss; he hates them so. If Roosevelt could say that he would give every kind of economic aid to the democracies, that might make an impression – but his hands are tied.'

The crisis passed; we gained our respite. Life and work went on as before. Which reminds me : what about my work? How could my career be said to be progressing?

Of my months at a desk in the Publications Department in a corner of the Palais des Nations, that vast, cream-coloured sprawl beside the lake, I can remember extraordinarily little. Only one piece of work successfully accomplished has stuck in my mind. A digest in English was required of one of the many pamphlets published in French for the Health Organisation and the virgin Unwin was set down to read, master and synthesise a detailed treatise on the Rehabilitation of Prostitutes.

Was Fritz behind this, I wonder? He must have felt I needed to broaden my mind.

Twelve

The warning hooter has sounded and, in company with a crowd of fellow cyclists, I am pedalling along a road in Old Woking. On one side of me the countryside has disappeared under Council housing estates; on the other the green fields are still inviolate, or nearly so. Out there, all on its own, straddling a small river and surrounded by playing fields and tennis courts, is a red-brick factory approached along a winding lane. This is Unwin Brothers, the family printing works, where I am learning the trade. Five days a week I arrive at half-past seven in the morning and, punctually with everyone else, leave nine hours later. As I have started in the composing room I spend almost the whole of this period on my feet, standing on a metal floor and fiddling with loose pieces of type; an invaluable preparation for the cocktail parties which I will attend later, and an aspect of my training which certainly would not have occurred to my father.

I am enjoying life at Woking. My job is interesting and practical, makes no intellectual demands and gives me visual scope. Lay-outs are just my line. I am taught the skills by a nice old compositor, approaching retiring age, who has spent his life in the firm. We are allowed a ten minute break in the morning and another in the afternoon, when we pull out drawers of type, sit on them and have a chat and a snack. Father is on the Board of Directors and I know he is critical of the way the place is run. (The quality of the work is excellent; it is the financial side which worries him.) I keep quiet about this, of course. I am very careful indeed not to put myself forward. I am trying to blend in and become a part of the place, but this is difficult to achieve. There are drawbacks. My name is one of them. Everyone is friendly but they make it clear that I am not, and can never hope to be, one of them and this I have to accept. The important thing is that I find them easy to get on with. They do not frighten me. I am boarding with one of the firm's proof readers and his family and feel completely at home there, although my ignorance of social mores left me hungry my first evening. Asked, on arrival, if I had had my tea, I said I had, thank you very much, then waited with ebbing confidence for the supper which never arrived.

The girls are a delight, aware of themselves sexually in an open, bracing way. They are great ones for badinage and ripe for teasing; excitingly yet never dangerously forward; strong on innuendo, never pushing things too far. We do not take advantage of each other. Without kissing, squeezing or even touching, a sufficiently stimulating time seems to be had by all. I spend hours with them on the firm's grass tennis courts, romping through the long summer evenings, and word gets back to Hampstead about it. My behaviour, my mother informs me, is out of place.

'Don't drag girls into the foreground more than you can help,' she writes. 'They are going to be useless to you in a year or two and if you go too far with them now they will only be an embarrassment to you in after years when you aren't feeling so enthusiastic. Dignity, dignity, with natural friendliness will always leave behind respect, but too much familiarity is not too good where stations in life are far apart. Not very socialistic I'm afraid, but we are not there yet!'

No doubt prompted by my parents, in an effort to divert me, one of my printing uncles invites me round to play tennis on his lawn in company with a group of young people of my own sort. A well-intentioned move, but doomed. These middle-class girls are, by comparison, hopelessly dull and formal. Accustomed to instant repartee, I find it impossible to get a smile or a rise out of them, and I expect they consider me insufferably brash. The attempt must have been seen to be a failure, for it is never repeated.

As the summer months go by, ignoring my parents' wishes, I become friends with a girl who works in the office and whose job it is to seek me out in whatever department I happen to be working and give me my post. These visits, at first infrequent, soon become daily occurrences. I am not, in fact, receiving a large number of outside letters. The correspondence she is now delivering to me consists almost entirely of letters from herself. 'You need not wonder why people like you, it is because you are always "David". So natural, always ready for a lark and yet a good listener, and above all full of sympathy. That is the best possible recipe for a character and you have it, bless you.'

We plan a day's outing together on our bicycles. I am riding ahead and whizzing fast down a steep Surrey hill when I hear behind me a sickening long-drawn-out scrape and grind of metal on tarmac. She has crashed. When I get back, I find her dazed and bewildered and bleeding from a gash in her scalp. Although neither she nor her machine is seriously damaged we need help, and luck is with us. Help is at hand, for we are no great distance from the home of my Brooke relations. So I escort her through the lodge gates and up the drive to the long, low Regency house set peacefully on its garden terrace with the lakes lying below and the beech woods rising behind. A posse of maids swiftly take charge of her and sweep her upstairs. My mother's old nurse is now living here and she takes me aside for a worried word. I do my best to reassure her. This is a friend from work. This is not the girl I intend to marry. She listens and nods her head but I can see she is still doubtful. Class is class, and who knows the divisions better, or adheres to them more firmly, than a life-long retainer?

I return my companion to her Council house later in the day and make my apologies to her parents. She is none the worse for the mishap and she has caught a glimpse of another and more privileged way of life, though whether she is any the better for it I would hesitate to say. I feel the experience is probably hard on her. News of *this* escapade is not long in reaching my father and mother and they react as I might have known they would; the older generation are curiously slow in adjusting to new ideas. They are still worried in case I compromise myself or do something stupid. Father is also aware of the girl's side of it. He keeps repeating helplessly, 'But you're a fairy prince!'

He had another plan for me for August and I found it an interesting prospect. I was to fly out to Hungary and work as a volunteer in a bookshop in Budapest. The family were to holiday in Liechtenstein, in a hotel in the mountains near Vaduz, and when my month's stint was over I was to join them there. The timing of these arrangements (the year was 1939) seems a little casual in retrospect. As we know, Father followed international events as keenly as most people and he was supposed to have his ear to the ground.

My friend from the office was not travelling to exotic parts. She was a Girl Guide and she had hoped to spend her summer holiday in a camp on the Devon coast. Now even these modest plans were in jeopardy. The problem was as simple as money – how complicated when you cannot lay your hands on it – and I wanted to help her. But *I* had no money either, since I was not earning anything, relying on my father for a small expense allowance. I forget what the sum was, perhaps ten or twelve pounds, probably less, but it was far beyond my means and I did not feel I could very well ask my family to produce it. Then a solution occurred to me. If, instead of flying, I took a train to Hungary, she might perhaps be given the money I had saved. I suggested the idea to my father and he instantly agreed.

This was exactly the kind of thoughtfully generous action he appreciated, for in spite of all his little economies and meannesses, his cheeseparing and his inability to 'splash', he was, in fact, a generous man. This is not understood. The world saw only his surface behaviour, which was often Scrooge-like. Tipping, for instance, was against his every instinct; he was the despair of waiters, page-boys and hotel lackeys. For some reason he seemed to feel it necessary to parade his parsimony : his charity he kept completely dark. Yet he was helping to support two of his brothers for large parts of their lives. He was constantly reaching into his purse to assist my more impecunious cousins with their education. Aware that he was, in financial terms, the most successful member of his family, he felt it his duty to assist the others and he did so gladly. A deserving author on hard times could equally be a recipient of his generosity, and not necessarily with any thought of future gains.

Thirteen

When my father was a young man of about my age and had gone to the Continent to master the complexities of the book trade, he had concentrated on the job. He had never, for a moment, allowed himself to be deflected from the task in hand. Tenacious, dedicated and determined, living on next to nothing, he had set me in those Leipzig days an example I should at least *attempt* to emulate.

> 'A most respected and centrally situated firm accepted me as a "volunteer" and there I worked for no pay for three and a half months from 8 in the morning until 8 at night, Saturdays included. They wanted me to work part of Sundays as well, but I was able to say with truth that my parents would have the strongest religious objections if I did so. The hours of work left little time for amusement. Moreover, on only two occasions could I put my hands upon the ninepence necessary to secure a seat at the opera. So short of money was I in those days that by the time I had paid my board at the Pension I could afford a penny cup of tea at the automatic restaurant next door on only one day in the week.'

I was familiar with his early struggles in Germany, for he had described them often enough. They were a part of the legend of his youth. He had sent me out to Budapest to profit – as he had profited – by my days as volunteer, to put my back into it and make the most of every minute of my time. But I found myself in a curious situation, it was all very difficult, my conscience troubled me, but what was I to do? This was not turning out as he had planned and he would most strongly disapprove should he ever find out about it, but was it my fault, I kept asking myself, if the owner of the book-shop *refused* to let me work?

I had dutifully arrived at opening time on my first day and again on my second. Then it was suggested that the weather was fine (which it certainly was) and that I must not spend all of every day indoors. I should go out and see something of their beautiful city. There were various young men on the staff who were ready to act as guides. This was true: their bright and eager faces surrounded me, they were longing for just such an opportunity. How could I dis-appoint them? It would be churlish to say no, and it was not in-tended that I should. Everyone was perfectly happy with the arrangement. They assumed that I had come to Hungary to enjoy myself, and I never did a stroke of serious work in the shop again.

Everywhere I went, to the Fun Fair dominated by its giant wheel, to Margareten Island, to the baths and swimming pools or to the parks with their open-air cafés and restaurants, I was accompanied by a group of lively young people, for my fellow assistants at the bookshop were quick to introduce me to their friends. As an Englishman, I found I enjoyed a certain *cachet* among them and their attentions warmed me. I was not accustomed to being sought after or listened to with such respect. We would order tall glasses of the light, cold lager beer and I grew fond of this refreshing drink and felt bold and rather daring when I drank it. On rare occasions, for it was a good deal more expensive, I might even have a nip of aromatic and fiery apricot brandy: the Hungarian speciality, *Barack*.

This was one part of my life. But there was another, equally dis-tracting, and this, too, had nothing whatever to do with work. The husband and wife in whose flat I was living were on uneasy terms. All they shared, in fact, was the roof. They went their separate ways. The wife looked after the business, a well-stocked bookshop in a fashionable street. She was a small, dark, good-looking woman in her mid-thirties, and her lover lived in the flat next door and was constantly in attendance. They, too, took me up – and out – and with them I visited glossier places of entertainment, night clubs

81

more exciting, even, than those described in *Queer Street*. (I *had* come a long way since leaving Geneva.)

The lover had a sister to whom I was introduced. She seemed agreeable enough and very willing to be friendly, but thirtyish and, from my viewpoint, middle-aged. Hints were dropped and grew broader, for I did not seem to be able to understand what was expected of me. I knew that she was unattached and at a loose end and thought this might explain why we were always being paired off together. In desperation, she took me to a tea dance at the Gelert Baths, where I shuffled her round the floor in time to the Palm Court orchestra, while she sparkled provocatively and pushed her soft chest against mine. Dimly, I felt I was being offered something. Was it a course of instruction? I had been sent here to acquire experience, but this had nothing to do with sales or discounts.

So the last hot August weeks of peace sped by, while unbeknown to my father I neglected my opportunities in every sense of the phrase. Abruptly the Soviet-German pact was signed. My friends were concerned; this was ominous news and they were all very sorry for me. In the days that followed it seemed clear that storm cones were being hoisted. My parents had arrived in Liechtenstein, they cabled me to join them, and I caught a plane on the last day of the month. There were frantic scenes at the airport, where people with a great deal to lose were trying to escape. We were buzzed by German fighter planes as we came in to land at Munich, but we were allowed to take off again and fly on to Lake Constance and safety. I had only just got away in time.

I found my family, anxious and isolated, in a hotel in a mountain village, and we were relieved to be re-united again. I lost no time in bringing out my gifts and souvenirs. Among them was a small china flask of *Barack*; a pretty little object decorated with a painting of apricots. Eager to show off, flaunting my new expertise, I opened it and passed it round. Everyone tried some; even my father was persuaded to take a sip. What a fuss he made! He really put on a show, choking, gagging, grimacing, spluttering with disgust, determined to demonstrate how nasty he thought it was. He had decided, I think, that this was his best defence, but I felt he was not taking me seriously and was hurt and annoyed.

The showdown came an hour or so later, at the evening meal. Father was holding the menu and ordering for everyone. He always did. I was not, of course, asked if I wanted to drink anything. (Sometimes we had fruit juice; at others a jug of water.) As the waiter turned away I signalled to him and ordered a bottle of beer. Now this may sound an unremarkable exercise on my part. A casual thing to do. In fact, it was momentous; it was apocalyptic. For the first time in my adult life I was showing initiative and daring to confront him. This was my first rebellious, independent move.

He did not attempt to countermand my order but sat there, silent and displeased. My bottle arrived and I drank it; deliberately challenging his authority. When we had finished the meal and were getting up from the table he walked round to me and in vehement, angry tones, in a voice of pent passion, hissed in my ear. 'I *hope* I am not going to *regret* having sent you to Budapest.'

I was not quite twenty-one years old.

Fourteen

Overshadowed by the shocks and traumas of domestic conflict, war was declared. We were in Zürich at the time. Father must have been caught (financially) short – an unusual occurrence – for he had had to borrow money from an obliging Swiss carpet dealer staying at our hotel in order to get us out of Liechtenstein. We must have been strolling in the town when the news reached us, for I remember my mother crying and retiring into a shop arcade to recover. All services through France were instantly suspended and it was not until three weeks later, together with several hundred other stranded travellers, that we boarded a special train at Geneva, taking with us provisions for forty-eight hours. We crossed the channel on an over-crowded vessel and arrived in London to find, instead of bombs and sirens, the unreal hiatus of the phoney war.

However, we had to be prepared. One of my father's most respected authors, Professor J. B. S. Haldane, had experienced air bombardment in the Spanish Civil War. A pickaxe, he informed us, was an essential item of equipment. With this tool, we should experience no difficulty in tunnelling our way out of the ruins of the home that had collapsed on top of us. My brother was instantly despatched into Hampstead to purchase the article and on his return we were faced with the problem – which was to remain with us until the end of hostilities – *where to put it?* The dining-room was sandbagged for our own use. Between it and the kitchen, both basement rooms, existed an airless, windowless space known as the wine cellar, although needless to say no wine had been stored there during my father's tenure of the house, and this was also pressed into service as a shelter. In time, however, we became increasingly casual and used it less and less. The only person I can recollect sleeping there was my French aunt, Uncle Jack's wife, up from the country and enduring her first raids.

The phoney war was a curious enough interlude, but even stranger, as the months wore on we were to find ourselves alone in the house. Every one of our living-in servants left us to take up war work of some kind. Never in my memory had those three small rooms on the top floor been unoccupied and now, suddenly, it was brought home to us that we would have to do things for ourselves. Father never adjusted happily. Mother, on the contrary, responded to the challenge. Then in her mid-fifties, she gamely took charge and, helped by Ruth, who gave her cooking lessons, proceeded to feed us all with increasing panache. There were failures, of course, and accidents. Putting some kind of laboriously contrived sloppy pudding into the refrigerator and slamming the door, she knocked the bowl over and spilled the contents. The mess oozed everywhere. Dancing about in the background – he still required his evening meal to be served at seven sharp and I suspect she must have been running late – my father was not much help. I remember him wringing his hands and exclaiming, 'Why don't you give us bread and cheese?'

As a family, we were to be out of step with the nation for the next five years, for none of us served in the armed forces. My father was too old, my brother too young, and I was classified as C3 when I went for my medical. I had 'registered' with other twenty-year-olds, in July, before my departure to Hungary. My health, once again, detached me from my generation and I was to live an odd, remote life, blocking myself off as far as I could – although this was not always possible, for I spent most of my time in London – from the realities around me. My mood continued to be almost wholly escapist.

On a fine afternoon at the end of September, soon after we had returned, I took a stroll across Hampstead Heath and took my Rolleiflex with me. Sand was being dug for sandbags and an enormous hole created, which was later to be filled with the pulverised remains of bombed houses. Searchlight and anti-aircraft gun emplacements had come into being since my last visit and there were soldiers about everywhere. I was not, however, a social historian and I had no interest in recording these transient phenomena. My eyes – and my camera – were fixed, as they always were, upon the eternal verities of nature. Absorbed in photography, I was startled among the beech trees in the grounds of Ken Wood by the pounding of boots and the next moment was surrounded by scarlet-faced militia. My film was confiscated and that evening we were visited by two rather sombre gentlemen from Scotland Yard. Father radiated confidence and reassurance; my press cuttings album was produced as proof of my innocence – I had been marketing my landscapes to the *Farmers' Weekly* and other journals since my schooldays – and since my negatives, in any case, showed nothing but clouds and branches I was let off with a caution. But the incident high-lights the degree of my non-involvement with the events of the time.

I returned to Unwin Brothers to complete my training; then left the printing works to join the staff of a well-known bookseller in a famous university city. Until the spring, I would be pedalling between my lodgings and the bookshop on Uncle Bernard's grey Sunbeam bicycle. Riding this machine, I had already encountered trouble in the Surrey hills. Now, riding to and fro among the spires and towers, I was to encounter trouble once again. Another golden head. A slim, attractive shape. One of the group of typists and secretaries who worked in the office upstairs. We kept company through that icy first winter of the war, and our relationship generated a gratifying degree of heat.

Perhaps because of the cold we became regular cinema-goers, and after the performance, when it was time to pedal back to our respective homes, we would walk along to the bookshop to collect our bikes. These we left, for safety, in the small shed alongside, where the staff garaged their machines. The street door of this shed was kept locked at night but I had been given a key to the shop itself, and we took our time about completing the comparatively short journey from the front door of the shop to the side door which opened into the cycle shed.

One night, we were observed. The owner of the shop happened

to be sitting in his car which was parked in the street opposite. He saw us enter and he waited for us to emerge. The minutes went by. He left his car, crossed the street and let himself in with his own key. The sound of the opening door shot us out of our burrow like a couple of startled rabbits. Seconds later, pushing our bicycles, we emerged on to the pavement to find our boss waiting for us. We were too abashed to do more than mumble goodnight to him and escape.

I did not feel I could ignore the incident, however, and sought him out next day to make my stammering apologies. I think he was surprised – certainly he raised an eyebrow – that I should be so concerned to bring the matter up. But I did not let it rest there. When I next went home I took my father into my confidence and spilled the beans to *him*. What problems, what embarrassments I caused him! And his was not the nature to ride them lightly. Always I seemed to be unburdening myself at his expense.

If I ended my career as a bookseller under a cloud, it was entirely of my own manufacture. I took my friend to Hampstead with me for a weekend at Easter and the visit was not altogether a success. Marriage was in neither of our heads, but once again this was not understood. My parents made me feel afterwards that I had not yet found Miss Right. I could have argued, I suppose, that my choice was restricted; the girls I met were the girls I worked with. I did ask them – for the problem appeared insuperable – where they thought I might find a *suitable* girl. Father was not stumped for an answer; he seldom was. He recommended the Friends Meeting House. Make a point, he said, of attending their services each Sunday.

My father and mother celebrated their silver wedding while I was at the bookshop and the letter I wrote to them has survived. In its artless, bouncy way it is not without interest for it shows that, tensions over the demon drink notwithstanding, I had remained an affectionate son.

'All the best wishes for a happy anniversary of your wedding to you, my sweet parents. What a marvellous couple you are! I often thank the Lord very loudly for my luck in not having been born into another family, the ——s for instance. You seem to have got the hang of me perfectly, so I think we can look forward to many more anniversaries as harmonious as this one; that is to say until I marry a kitchenmaid or an earl's daughter or something and upset things a little.'

My stint at the bookshop ended in the spring and I spent the summer, Dunkirk summer, 'on the road', lugging a heavy suitcase of Phaidon publications into bookshops in every corner of the British Isles. I was not to learn a great deal about the techniques of selling, for those art books sold themselves. Orders had to be rationed. However, I was greeted as my father's son, with great friendliness, by booksellers from Perth to Penzance; Carlisle to Canterbury. I visited industrial centres, university towns, cathedral cities; staying in commercial hotels where I was appalled by the tales told by my colleagues. I had not encountered really dirty stories before.

While on my travels, I spent one hot and sunny weekend at a farmhouse in Essex. Here I found myself where I was always happiest, in the centre of a group of lovely girls. The weather, the place, the company conspired to entrap me. I was enjoying it all so much that, when a flawless Monday morning dawned, I could not tear myself away.

Father learnt that I had taken a day off and he was profoundly shocked. This was heresy. Dr Horovitz of the Phaidon Press was my employer at the time, and I was letting him – and my father – down. He did not point out, and he might with justice have done so, that my contemporaries, few of whom were in my favoured position, would have faced a court martial for an equivalent breach of their duty.

Tingates, the Essex farmstead where I had shamefully succumbed to temptation, was to play a crucial role in my life – and subsequently in Rayner's. Isobel lived here with her step-mother (now divorced from Harold Curwen) and her two younger step-sisters.

It was with these girls that I had been swimming in the millstream when I ought to have been on the road as a 'rep'. Tingates was to be instrumental in providing me, not only with friends (that essential other social group, apart from my family) but in due course with a career and a wife, although I left it to my brother to marry one of the daughters of the house. And what a charming place it was, welcoming, warm, wonderfully eccentric; a toy farm with barns, stables and pigsties growing out of the southern slope of a peaceful river valley.

That first weekend in high summer was followed by others, but my bond with Tingates was finally cemented in the autumn of 1940, when the bombing began in earnest. Father had planned for me to start work at the firm in September, but I suspect that my mother sabotaged the idea, probably feeling that her cracked pot was safer out of London. In all events, I was granted yet another respite from office life and I spent the months until Christmas in a trance of happiness assisting on the farm. I had been at school in the country, had gone for walks in the country, and I had read my Adrian Bell, but this was my first-ever taste of genuine country life. Donning a stout pair of agricultural breeches, I turned my hand to everything; I learnt to pluck and dress chickens – and wring their necks – feed the pigs, milk cows and goats, deal with livestock, plant vegetables, handle a shot gun, drive the pony cart and ride a horse. What an education I was given! I became a part of the place; a member of the household. I soon felt more at home there than I felt at home.

My parents, too, were to find a refuge at the farm for a few weeks that autumn. A large time bomb just missed our house and fortunately failed to explode, but its arrival in our neighbour's garden necessitated a prompt move out of danger. They settled at Tingates and my father caught a train daily to London, driving off each morning in his town suit, leaving me labouring enjoyably in my working clothes, my hands stained black with walnut juice. (We had had a bumper crop and bagged up several sacks of nuts to sell in the market.) But sadly enough, neither he nor my mother really fitted in. It was not just that country life did not work for them; my father never appreciated staying with other people. He always seemed a lost being, casting around desperately for a base in a strange room, unable to relax properly without his accustomed chair, table and small sewing cabinet with the drawer for his sweets, and finding himself unable to adapt smoothly to a routine which was not his own. Yet he continued to the end to speak nostalgically of his days on the farm in the wilds of South Africa and New Zealand and of the rural delights – ploughing with fourteen donkeys was one of them – he had enjoyed on his world tour as a young man.

One episode which stems from this period has no bearing on country life in East Anglia but is interesting, for it reveals my father in a deeply intractable mood. He was not quick to take offence but, once convinced in his mind that a wrong had been done, he would find it impossible ever to forgive the guilty party. Such a degree of inflexibility could lead to tricky social moments and point-blank refusals on his part to meet, greet or in any way recognise the presence of a person whose conduct, in his judgement, had not been 'straight' or honourable. One of Harold Curwen's business partners happened to be just such a man. The rights and wrongs of the long-ago issue are no concern of mine. For some reason he had incurred my father's disapproval; he was plainly *persona non grata,* and this made things extremely difficult when he called at the farm one day. Father's swift and determined evasive action left us all stunned and amazed.

As soon as it was safe for them to do so, my parents returned to Hampstead and I continued with my simple country life. Isobel had joined the Fannys and I saw her only occasionally, but the youngest of the Curwen sisters had become a friend. She was thirteen years old and growing rapidly tall; a diffident and awkward schoolgirl (reminding me of her father) but beautiful, with delicate colouring and a mane of tawny hair, and I found peace and a contented tranquillity in her companionship.

I was peaceful, I am sure, because I was satisfied and because I was entirely happy in my life. For a change, I had not been dumped somewhere and told to get on with it. I no longer needed distractions. I was at Tingates by my own choice. Tingates was the one place in the world where I really wanted to be.

Fifteen

My hands are clean again and I am sitting at my desk in the Production Department at Allen & Unwin, busy with the layout of a jacket. *A Tale of Internment* is the title of the book and I am playing around with the author's head, or should I say a photograph of the author's head? She is a striking blonde and makes frequent calls at the office to see my cousin Philip. This, in the manner of offices, gives rise to facetious comment and time-checks are made on the duration of her visits. Good-natured teasing is very much a part of our routine. I indulge in it myself.

Wartime restrictions are, of course, a bugbear and paper is strictly rationed. We have our quota and, as a solidly respectable, old-established firm, we do not buy on the open market, which exists and which supports the mushroom growth of small new publishing businesses, disapproved of by Father and owned for the most part by newcomers from central Europe. However, we *are* occasionally tempted to acquire a little on the side. I have just come out of the Chairman's lavatory with a really splendid piece of early forties toilet paper; dim brown and speckled like a wild bird's egg with multi-coloured dots. Carefully I cut off the perforations and clip to it a note that I have been lucky enough to be able to purchase so and so many reams of this sample at such and such a price. This I leave on the production manager's desk and wait with eager anticipation his return from lunch. His horrified start and clap of hand to the top of his head are ample reward for my efforts. Needless to say, I am quick to set his mind at rest.

The Art Editor, whose place I am filling, is a Conscientious Objector and he is out in the country, where I would like to be, working on a farm. I have had to abandon *my* farm during the week to work in London. The bombing had not ended, but it was more sporadic, and we have to move valuable items, manuscripts, the bulky stock books, down into a fireproof safe in the basement every evening and fetch them out again in the morning; a necessary chore. The business has already suffered a bad loss when a warehouse in which our printed sheets were stored was gutted in an air raid. The figures, which still ring in my mind, became as the years went on an incantation. Father never tired of repeating them. I think the syllables had a soothing effect on him, for he had taken the blow philosophically. 'In that one night we lost one million four hundred thousand books affecting two thousand one hundred titles on our list.'

Now and again I was able to use one of my own photographs on a book jacket or on the cover of a spring or autumn list, and when this happened I paid myself at the going rate. I had bought an enlarger and was producing exhibition-sized prints in my bedroom darkroom. Buying the instrument was, I remember, a saga in itself for my father came with me, and I found his manner with shop assistants embarrassing. Perhaps I am thin-skinned, but it has never been quite as essential to me – as it obviously was to him – to attempt to drive down the price. (Bargaining was so engrained in his nature that he tended to behave in the West End of London as if he were shopping in Port Said.) I needed a good enlarger for the type of work I wanted to do, but the cost made him whistle. I am astonished, at this remove, that I could not afford the tenner out of my own pocket, without having to involve him. I may have been overcome with the gravity of the purchase and had asked him to come along and back me up. This is perfectly possible, for I was to consult him over money matters for as long as he lived. Finance provided a foothold; a meeting ground where we could tread with ease.

I set up the enlarger on a trestle table between my two blacked-out windows, and an excellent distraction it proved to be. Sirens might sound, guns hammer and bombs fall, but perched up there on the first floor of our tall house I was too absorbed to pay attention, while on the floor below my parents would continue to sit in front of the radiogram, drowning out the racket with a record of Dvorak's New World Symphony played at top volume.

Photography was my pastime : I knew I would never make it my career. What I *had* discovered I wanted to do, and with passion, was to write. As the son of my father, I could hardly have made a more tactless choice. He was a professional, an expert; who knew better than he the odds against success? True, a few, a very few authors made a satisfactory living from their books, but there were far more who did not. As for the unpublished and unpublishable, they were a multitude. They all thought they could write and their typescripts poured into the office. Out of this slush pile of un-solicited MSS, possibly once in a year – or once in two years – a gleaming nugget might emerge. I knew this. One of my duties was to cast an eye over the pile – for every typescript submitted, how-ever small and battered, was carefully scrutinised – and set aside any I thought looked promising. I remember gems to this day; verses which would certainly earn a place in a Stuffed Owl anthology.

'And what are we?' demanded one would-be poet, 'but little sugar lumps,/Dropped from the tongs of time into life's tea,/There to dissolve and sweeten it for God?' (I have always found this a movingly *British* view of the human situation.) Yes, I knew the odds were unfavourable, but this could not deter me. An author I was quite determined to be. The snag was, I had not yet decided exactly what it was that I was so determined to write.

Every attempt I made was as hopeless as the last. For days I struggled with a short piece about a silver birch tree, crawling up to my subject like a caterpillar and browsing on it voraciously for three or four pages until I had stripped it of every conceivable angle of interest. Inspecting my efforts afterwards, I realised sadly that it was not just unsaleable; it was unreadable. One more dollop of sludge for the heap. The idea of an adult audience, lying in wait out there and ready to demolish me, paralysed my mind and cramped my writing style. In spite of my years I was not grown-up, or did not feel so. How could I match myself against this mythical circle of readers ringing me round; all so knowledgeable, so intelligent, such sophisticates? How could I escape my inadequacy? A solution suddenly occurred to me. Why not write for boys and girls instead?

My material was there to hand: the farm I loved so much and the country around it. In the early autumn of 1941 a new family had moved into a converted (but primitive) barn that lay a short distance below Tingates. The Herberts had a young daughter and instead of one companion to enliven my weekends, I now had two. What could be simpler than to put them in a book?

I began my story and the words flowed easily, no longer tense and congealed. I had an urge to proselytise, to sing the praises of the English countryside, to reach out to children – and there were enormous numbers of them – locked away in the big cities and unable to escape. The year before, a small group of evacuees, children and their mothers, were billeted on us at Tingates; East-Enders who were taking the brunt of the bombing in the Blitz. We made them as comfortable as we could on the hay in the barn, and I have never forgotten their excitement and wonder at everything they saw around them, for it so exactly matched my own.

I wrote in the evenings; I took the manuscript to the office with me and wrote it at my desk, and I thought and dreamed about it all week long. Then, in two or three months, it was finished. What next? Father had dropped no word of encouragement and had looked on a little dourly. Here was a development which he could not but deplore. He was absolutely right, of course, not to build up my hopes, and in fact his reserve did not worry me. I was confident that the world would welcome my offering. Amazingly enough, in my case, I was not disillusioned.

I had decided to write under a pseudonym, for it really was vital that I should keep my identity dark. No one must be able to say to me, of course *you* can get your books published. I chose my grandmother's maiden name, Severn, for this was a family connection I was proud of. (Joseph Severn, the painter, had accompanied John Keats to Rome and had cared for the poet until he died.) The typescript, then, under my pen-name, was sent to a children's editor whose opinion my father respected and she returned it with a favourable report. I was over the first hurdle. He was now prepared to give me qualified support.

He was a part owner of the publishing house of John Lane The Bodley Head at that time, and they had some good children's authors on their list. (The firm was conveniently situated in Bury Place, only a few steps away from Ruskin House, and after he had read the post and dealt with urgent matters at Allen & Unwin he would pop across to The Bodley Head, which he was managing through a manager.) Off went my book to them, again anonymously, and was accepted on its merits. Father was at last convinced. At once, like a battleship, guns swivelling, he swung into line behind me and prepared to fire broadsides on my behalf.

I was in an absurdly favourable position. No other young author – I was not yet twenty-four – could have hoped to have had such a strategically-placed 'honorary agent' as my publishing parent. He decided the terms of my contracts; he allocated the supply of paper which, in the case of juveniles during the war, virtually determined the sales. There was a shortage of children's books and you sold the number of copies you printed. It was as easy as that. My first book got a reasonable welcome and my second a better one, but it was the situation, not the reviews, that was the key to my success. This was perhaps not as apparent to me as it should have been. I published a book a year for the next ten years and the first five showed mounting sales. From 1947 onwards came the inevitable decline. However, it was a good ride while it lasted and my metamorphosis into David Severn transformed my life. I had no financial bent and it still seemed to me very, very doubtful if I would be capable of fending for myself out there on the ocean of life. As for the sheltered waters of the family harbour; the harbour-master was too much of a dominant character to make this anchorage attractive. Suddenly, I was presented with the freedom of the seas.

My extravagant good fortune went, I think, more to my agent's head than to my own. Thanks to his generosity I was soon enjoying 20% royalties, large editions and a handsome income. I was sitting on a bandwagon and there were others eager to join me. The manager of the Bodley Head – a man in a most invidious position

– had his own friends and protégés to support, and when they duly sent in their manuscripts their contracts were drawn up on similar lines to my own. This was not at all what my father had intended! He had to gun them down. He had taken the firm over in order to build it up – it was in a poor state when he had acquired it – and he was accepting no fees for his services. He saw my inflated royalties as an overdue reward for the work he was putting in gratis. There was no reason why strangers should benefit. I was outside the zone of conflict but reverberations reached me, and I did not improve the situation by sending in a 'thumbs down' reader's report on one of the new juveniles submitted.

I became, then, in those war years, an inconsiderable deity in the pantheon of children's writers. And what strange Gods were worshipped there! Lewis Carroll, Kenneth Graham, James Barrie; oddities, all of them. I suppose I, too, could be said to be an oddity : shunning my own age-group; content to spend my time in the company of schoolgirl friends. Schoolgirls make a habit of growing up, however, and as the next chapter will demonstrate, I was soon to be my more normal self again.

Sixteen

The rhythm of life continued, uninterrupted by the shower of gold. My job in the production department was treated as a contribution of a kind to the war effort and while health and strength lasted – and I enjoyed a run of three uninterrupted years! – I continued to design my books. But there was no longer any question of my making publishing a career. I had removed myself in spirit, if not yet in body, from George Allen & Unwin and my future independence was recognised, although it was never discussed. My brother was growing up and I think my father was already swivelling his sights on to this more lively and promising target for his hopes.

I would like to be able to report that my literary success had smoothed our personal relations, but in truth I cannot do so. I should not, of course, have still been living at home. For five and a half days of every week – for we worked on Saturday mornings – I was subject to my father's timetable, and the fact that I was now financially free and, perhaps more importantly, had become a person in my own right, made me if anything more intolerant and impatient than before. I was developing a hatred of cities and of London in particular. On sunny, blue-sky days I found it a physical agony to be shackled to my desk. I lived for the weekends and my escape into the countryside.

Tingates, however, was no longer the centre of my universe. I slept up there and I had most of my meals up there; ostensibly, I still belonged with the Curwens. But the wavering compass needle of my affections was on the move again and more and more of my time was spent with those recently arrived neighbours, the Herberts who lived in The Barn.

The war, which had left our family unscathed, had already in

1942 stripped them of their men. There remained a widow and two daughters, the elder of whom was a nurse in a hospital in York. The presence of the younger girl drew me down the hill, where I was soon locked in loving combat with the mother. Staunch, indomitable, bearing up bravely under a rain of blows, I can best describe Molly as a militant pacifist. She and my father were both socialists and had much in common. She had, like him, definite opinions about almost everything, and she held to them quite as firmly as he did and expressed them just as forcefully. In many ways she was his female counterpart, which may explain why they could not become friends but, keeping at a little distance, regarded each other with. tempered respect. My arguments with her were usually sparked off by an article or editorial in *Peace News*, a newspaper she subscribed to and whose views I could not tolerate. Periwinkle sat, a withdrawn figure during these joustings, occupied with homework or a book.

How the Herberts came to be here after many wanderings, with their good pieces of Georgian furniture and their Persian rugs spread over the concrete floor – across which, in wet weather, streamed a small river of rainwater – has no place in this story, but their arrival was timely. My life, a short while ago such a muddle and perplexity, was swiftly gaining direction and a shape.

Molly was the most unfussed and unfussing of parents. She trusted me with her daughter, who became my constant companion. We rode together or hid ourselves away in some private corner of the water meadows, where I read aloud to her or discussed poetry and books. We never spoke of love and I never touched her. I saw our relationship as infinitely precious and fragile; as delicately poised as a reflection in still water and as easily fractured by a rough or careless move. Not until she was sixteen, young enough in all conscience, did we declare ourselves to each other. Afterwards, we took only Molly into our confidence.

My parents must have been aware of what was happening; the Herberts were growing visibly into my life. But nothing was said. Perhaps they were deliberately taking no notice, in the hope that the problem might soon go away. Certainly, they were not going to

99

stand up and applaud. In their eyes, Periwinkle was much too young. Meanwhile, they saw us together, for I encouraged her up to London, unknown territory as far as she was concerned. Those were the years of that useful social leveller : the five shilling meal. This was the maximum price you were permitted to pay for your food; classier places could add a half-crown cover charge. So I took my sixteen-year-old to Claridges' 'Causerie' restaurant, where for seven shillings and sixpence a head we ate our fill from the cold buffet; then on to the Aeolian Hall for an afternoon's poetry reading by poets, organised by the Sitwells and attended by the Queen and the young princesses.

Her sister, at this stage in the war, was engaged to an airman and, predictably, he was killed. The word reached Essex on a day when Molly and her elder daughter were in London, and Freda Curwen telephoned my father at his office. Unhesitatingly, he responded and laid aside his work. A call to duty, however painful, always brought out the best in him. And when he died, twenty-five years later, Penelope wrote that 'my own most grateful and poignant memory of him goes back to the time in 1943 when he so kindly came and hunted us out at the National Gallery to break the news of Charles being reported missing, and saved me getting the shattering news when I got back to York that night. It was a wonderful bit of tact and kindness.'

Reverting to our own affairs, when we finally told my parents of our engagement they did not react as I had hoped. They were sitting by themselves in the dining-room – quite why, I cannot remember; perhaps *we* had occupied the drawing-room – and I took Periwinkle in with me and announced that we were going to be married. There was a moment's petrified silence; my mother looked horrified and my father's head slumped forward as if I had hit him; his beard pressed into his chest. Mother, after a brief but obvious hesitation, pulled herself together and opened her arms for an embrace, but my father continued to stare glumly at the table. He did not lift his head or move or say a word.

Her youth was bound to tell against her, for my health had been giving trouble again and it was too much to expect my parents willingly to entrust their precious invalid to the care of a child. We announced our engagement in 1944, and I spent the whole of that year at home in a grey gloom of weakness and depression. If my heart condition was largely psychological – and it certainly became so – I am puzzled why I should have collapsed at this point, when everything was going so well for me. This last of my major break-downs – my health was to heal wonderfully after my marriage – followed a five-mile walk to the farm one evening, after I had missed a bus connection. The effort was apparently too much for me, my heart began its uncontrollable thumping, and for months afterwards the slightest exertion would set it hammering again. All through this period it was a constant and boring partner, sharing my life, never quiet, hampering activity by day and at night setting the bed springs creaking with its strident beat. My symptoms were alarming but our family doctor was, I think, too easily alarmed. He certainly succeeded in lowering my parents' spirits. They obviously regarded me, at this time, as a chronic invalid, in no sense a suitable marriage partner for a robust young woman.

Did they feel it was their duty to impress upon my bride-to-be the gravity of the task that lay ahead of her? Were they making a last-ditch bid to deflect us from our intentions? I think it would be fairer to assume that they were acting protectively towards us both. Whatever the reasoning behind it, an interview was arranged. Peri-winkle was to have a talk with my doctor, and at this interview he told her to consider carefully before she married me because, in his opinion, I had not many years to live.

A stiff dose of medicine for a teenager! Death had already touched her more than once; she had lost her adored brother, and it is a tribute to her determination and strength of mind that she did not let his verdict discourage her. She took the problem to her sister who, with her medical background, was able to reassure her a little. I was told nothing of all this, and not until many years later did I hear the story.

We went ahead with our wedding plans and I had largely, if not completely, recovered when we were married. By then my parents were resigned, or prepared at any rate to accept the inevitable.

Father wrote us one of his 'instant' letters on the evening of his return from the wedding.

'Everyone seems to think that todays proceedings were highly satisfactory and I hope that you two were equally satisfied. This is just to let you know that you are much in our thoughts; that we hope the White Horse has proved to be to your liking and that your honeymoon may be a peculiarly happy one.

Well, you are embarking upon a great adventure which calls for the best in you both. There is nothing in life more worth while making a success of and you will have the good wishes and the prayers of
your devoted Daddy,
Stanley Unwin.'

While Periwinkle and my mother came quickly to love each other, I cannot say that my father ever really warmed to her (or, for that matter, she to him). He was, of course, always loyal and supportive. Now and again, at book trade and other functions, he would run into her literary uncle. The Herbert family, however, had suffered an unfortunate rift, and APH had never met, and nor was he curious to hear about, his niece. To my father, this was unthinkable – the family was all-important – and Alan Herbert's attitude never ceased to baffle him. Over the years, he made several attempts to stimulate interest in the connection and reported each failure with puzzled regret.

When, in the late fifties, we suffered a minor car crash and Periwinkle's face was very slightly scarred, he encouraged her as 'a handsome woman' to claim damages, a move which had not occurred to either of us. But their warmest moment of rapport undoubtedly came at the very end of his life, when she took a temporary job in Selfridge's toy department during the months before Christmas. She was forty years old and had not been employed before. She was told at the Labour Exchange that she was jumping in at the deep end, but in fact she was a success and enjoyed herself immensely. As a by-product, she found herself for the first time the focus of my father's attention. Not only did he respect her initiative; he was keenly curious to hear about her experiences. Trade, after all, was in his blood.

Seventeen

The break with my parents had come late – I was in my twenty-seventh year – and was felt all the more keenly. My mother was in tears on the doorstep when I took my final leave. But I needed to get away: I was being smothered by care and concern. Mother always organised everything for us down to the smallest detail and the menfolk were not expected to lift a domestic finger. My father, for instance, never packed for himself. I had received a more bracing education on the farm, where I was often the only man in a gathering of up to a dozen women. This was a balance I approved of but, rarity that I was, I was still not permitted to slack. I had been over-indulged at home, however, as Perwinkle was to find when she married me. What was the cause of our first tiff and tears? The airing of my pyjamas. No wonder she referred caustically to my brother and myself as 'two kidneys embedded in fat!'

I was now living an independent married life in the west country, far away from London, but I wrote incessantly to Hampstead and my letters – which were preserved – are full of boring domestic minutiae. For so long had our close entanglement lasted, that I still needed to involve them in every smallest detail of my new existence. Father, writing to my brother earlier in the year – Rayner was now in the Navy, on board a Tank Landing Ship in Far Eastern waters – had more vital matters to report. One letter in particular, dated 5 January 1946, is a chant of delight:

'On the 8th December (Sat) after I had just taken Mummy up some tea (she was ill in bed) the postman pressed into my hands a long white envelope O.H.M.S. marked Urgent, Personal and Confidential, with the words

Prime Minister printed in the bottom corner. I did not open it at once because I had an intuitive feeling about what it contained. The enclosed letter read : – Sir, I am desired by the Prime Minister to inform you that it is his intention, on the occasion of the forthcoming list of New Year Honours, to submit your name to the King with a recommendation that he may be graciously pleased to approve that the honour of Knighthood be conferred upon you etc etc.

On the ground that (a) the news was confidential (b) that there's many a slip twixt cup and lip (c) it might send Mummy's temperature up yet further, I laid low and said nothing until New Year's Eve when a congratulatory telegram from Aberdeen came through on the telephone. Mummy said what are they congratulating us about? Is some other Scottish university granting you a degree? I replied that in Scotland they celebrated New Year not Christmas, but Mummy retorted Yes, but we don't congratulate people at Christmas, a fact which I could not deny. After that I had to break the news to her. Her comment was, Well we shall have to try *to live it down*! The following morning it was announced both on the 7 o'clock and the 8 o'clock news. I was one of the few out of about 60 knights whom they mentioned. All the papers (except the News Chronicle) gave my name. The Times and Telegraph had the full list of all the Honours. The Birmingham Post and Manchester Guardian picked me out for special mention in their leading articles and there are pleasant references in Time and Tide, the New Statesman and other weeklies.

Within 5 minutes of 8 o'clock the telephone began to ring. Then the telegrams flowed in by the score, followed by letters, hundreds of them. I have acknowledged about 200 telegrams and letters and am only about a third of the way through. Some of the messages are wonderful and the variety of people incredible from Lord Moran (Churchill's Doctor) and Lord Horder to Cabinet Ministers like Stafford Cripps and Pethwick Lawrence. Prof. G. M. Trevelyan wrote a most appreciative letter which in itself was an honour to receive. But I should weary you if I enumerated them all . . . and still they pour in.

I must say that it is quite amusing to be addressed 'Sir Stanley' and to see the letters arrive for Sir Stanley Unwin LLD which is now correct, or rather will be after I have been to Buckingham Palace. Meanwhile The Trustees of the National Portrait Gallery have the honour to inform Sir Stanley Unwin that they wish to include his photograph in the National Record of Distinguished Persons (a fact which Lady Unwin finds difficult to believe) and Debrett want full details of Sir Stanley's ancestry etc for their next issue. Well, that's about all except that Sir Stanley would like to hear that you are not unduly shocked by the news. Most of the letters talk about the honour as long overdue or belated.'

Father had a thirst for recognition and lapped up honours like a bibulous socialite gulping champagne. He became twice a knight when he got his KCMG, and amassed a collection of foreign decorations; Palmes en Or from Belgium, White Lions from Czechoslovakia and Falcons from Iceland. There is no doubt that they made him very happy. Praise and appreciation, too, went to his head like strong drink and on occasion euphoria fuddled his logic, as in this epistle to my mother from New York, written in 1927, soon after his *Truth* was published in the States. 'Today, Thursday, I was entertained by the Publishers' Luncheon Club. They had *all* read my book! and were most excited about it. Every publisher is full of praises and all say how much they have learnt. Several have even gone so far as to say they have learnt more from it than they ever knew before.'

He attached an almost mystical importance to his name and, even when we were children, he was never simply our 'devoted Daddy' but always ended his letters to us with his signature. The meteoric rise to fame of *another* Stanley Unwin, the radio comedian, who rapidly became the more widely known, really upset him, and no doubt he was relieved to acquire a nicely balanced pair of handles, not merely as an adornment to those two very special words but to ensure that they remained to some extent unique. As was to be expected, he deplored the increasingly common use of Christian names among acquaintances, feeling that these should be reserved strictly for intimates. Apart from members of his family circle – of his own generation or older – very few people indeed were permitted to call him 'Stanley', while he, in turn, rigidly eschewed the habit. This led to occasional absurdities, as when writing to his friend the Lord Provost of Edinburgh, he found himself addressing him as 'My dear Darling.'

Father was an ambitious man. What made him so? Money was not essentially the motive; he wanted more than financial success. He liked to stress his family's poverty but, as my cousin Philip points out, this was comparative rather than actual, since his Spicer mother was handsomely endowed. The family printing works were destroyed by fire in 1895, when he would have been a boy of ten, an impressionable age, but it seems nearer the truth that it was my grandfather's 'rigid determination never to give less than one eighth of his income to good causes, plus the heavy mortgage and upkeep of his vast Victorian home near Bromley, which made him seem permanently hard up until his old age'.

This suburban mansion, with its attendant vine and orchid houses, gave my father a life-long horror of 'glass'. He was also deterred from owning a house until he was in his seventies. He always leased his various homes and his advice to us children, when we grew up, to do the same took no account of the changing post-war scene. Interestingly enough, in the years shortly after his death, both my sister and I were to embellish our gardens with conservatories, although without the dire results which no doubt he would have predicted had he been alive!

While on his world tour in 1913, before they were even engaged, he gives my mother a sober résumé of his financial situation:

'I may be proud but I am not sensitive about money affairs for I have nothing of which to be ashamed. By dint of jolly hard work and considerable economy I accumulated £1,300. It took some doing I can assure you! £1,000 is invested in various directions. The odd £300 I am devoting to making the present trip. I know I shall probably want every penny of capital I can put my hands on when I return. At the same time I know this trip is an unique experience and of the utmost value to me. I look upon the money expended as invested in myself.'

And a very sound investment he made of it.

While my father had financial acumen, which he enjoyed using, he never employed it as an end in itself. He could have stayed in the city and made his pile, no doubt, without a great deal of difficulty, but he would have been ashamed to have done so. He disapproved in principle of the idea of money making money, although he was prepared to make use of it, but unearned incomes were another matter. As children, we were brought up to expect nothing and we would have received very little indeed in the way of capital had it not been pointed out to him, when he had reached an advanced age and was still the sole owner of the firm, that unless a distribution was made, and made quickly, the business would founder under a weight of death duties.

He soon succeeded financially. What he had to struggle towards, and perhaps never completely attained, was social repose. There was a chip on his shoulder; a very slight one perhaps, but in some contexts he was strangely uncertain of himself. I have suggested already that he had difficulty in relating to people, and he was often socially maladroit. But there was more to it than that. He was dogged by a sort of middle-class malaise; a queasiness that called for soothing syrups and for which knighthoods, honorary degrees and decorations seemed a proper prescription.

I have mentioned earlier that, before the war, we lived opposite the Fabers. Geoffrey Faber was a university man. More importantly, he was a Fellow of All Souls. Now this fact was very often referred to by my father, and in slightly wistful terms, not altogether untinged with envy. As a Fellow of All Souls, he appeared to suggest, you were safe and beyond competition. Once elected, there you sat, like a bust in an alcove, in a coveted social niche. Yet at the same time, and contradictorily, he could make it clear that he did not approve of further education and that Oxford and Cambridge were poor substitutes for that much superior institution, the University of Life.

This draws me to relate a searing incident of his youth. He told me the story only once, and then in a tone of voice which made it instantly clear that he had been branded, and that the scar had only partially healed. A necessary step in his life's advancement, he felt, was to belong to one of the larger and more important of the London clubs. Accordingly, one morning in his lunch hour, he went into the club of his choice, produced his card and asked the porter at the door if he could see the Secretary. He was instantly swept off into the recesses of the building, following the porter through doors and down passages, at first impressed by the speed at which events were shaping – possibly, after all, he was a better known figure than he had given himself credit for – and then growing slowly disillusioned as it became clear that he had left the comfortable members' quarters behind and was now traversing the bleaker service regions of kitchens and storerooms. In the end, he landed up in front of the butler's desk, for it had been assumed by the porter that he was a representative of Unwins, the well-known firm of wine merchants. Father was not secure enough to laugh off the error. His shame and humiliation were such that he walked straight out of the building and when, after many years, he had recovered sufficiently to make a second attempt, he did not return there but became a member of another club.

Ten years without living-in servants went by before my parents decided to make life a little easier for themselves by moving out of the basement of their house. Until the autumn of 1949, my mother cooked in the large, dark kitchen and we continued to use the small room at the back – originally a servants' hall – as a dining-room. Now they were at last installing a kitchen on the ground floor and bringing into use again the original dining-room, never used as such and still referred to by everyone as 'the nursery'. (Rayner, the last incumbent, was now nearly twenty-five years old!) I think the delay was largely due to my father's reluctance to lose his study, a room which housed his roll-top desk but which he was hardly known to use, invariably doing his work in the drawing-room. Here he is, writing to my brother and bemoaning his fate :

> 'This has been a mournful Sunday for me, despite the sunshine. I have spent it removing the last of my belongings from the only study of my own I have ever had, or I suppose am now ever likely to have, and I could have wept. The door to the sitting room which I had made when we took the house is now boarded up and the tiles behind the sink will be fixed tomorrow. Thereafter the carpenter and painters will get busy. It has been a hectic week for Mummy with days when she was providing tea to two gas men in the basement, two plasterers in my study, a telephone man in the nursery and Collyer in the garden, after which she got some for herself and I came in for the wash-up !'

When he had a book to write or a new edition to revise, far from making use of his own study he would head north and stay at the St Deiniol's Residential Library, founded by Gladstone near his home at Hawarden, Chester, where 'for an additional shilling a day over and beyond most modest charges for board, one is provided with a private study where one can work completely undisturbed. This place is quite entertaining,' he writes to Rayner.

> 'Thoroughly Anglo-Catholic, with five services a day in their own chapel which I am afraid I do not attend and grace in Latin before and after meals, with much crossing oneself. The punctuality is incredible. It is rather like being back at school. If you leave your room the second the bell goes you are late and liable to a severe reprimand from the Warden, who is standing to attention at his place waiting to say grace before the bell has stopped ringing. Meals are taken at an amazing tempo and before the last mouthful is swallowed the Warden is standing to attention again.
> 'A person who was twenty seconds late for breakfast was so severely ticked off that I was afraid I should over-

sleep one morning, and sure enough I did. The first thing I heard was the breakfast bell. Had I been dressed and *run* down I should have been late. But I was neither washed nor dressed and to arrive six minutes late would cause such a stir and lose me so much face that it could not be contemplated. What was I to do? What would *you* have done? I am afraid that I was very naughty and remembering (a) that I had an apple in my drawer (b) that it is a very Catholic establishment, dressed quickly and went down to my study near the dining hall. A minute later, when I heard the Warden pass, I emerged (from my strenuous early morning labours!) and said, "I am fasting this morning. I take it that is all right?" and received, instead of a reprimand for unpunctuality, a beatific smile and "Oh, certainly." Thus in the most shameful fashion plucking credit for virtue. You will now understand why I was never found out at school. However, I am confessing to you because confession is good for the soul.'

*

Ruth had married early in the war and my mother and father were now grandparents. She had a family of four; three of them boys. This would have pleased him more had they been Unwins; unfortunately, so far as he was concerned, they bore their father's name. We had a boy and a girl and were disinclined to add to their number. Then Rayner married Carol Curwen and a son arrived and afterwards a daughter. Bolder than us, they continued and now it was Carol's turn to produce a pair of twins. I was with my father when he heard the news of their arrival. Two girls! This was a sad blow and he could not conceal his disappointment. However, in spite of a meagre ration of Unwin grandsons, he would be consoled to know that both the young men have joined the family firm.

Eighteen

We bought our first dwelling for five hundred pounds: a cottage above the river Wye. Father and Mother used to drive down to see us and, because we had no spare room, they would stay in Monmouth at the Beaufort Arms Hotel. I remember one particularly animated evening with my father in top form, dominating the conversation throughout dinner and again in the lounge afterwards. I was content to sit and listen and I hardly said a word. Later, when we had departed and they were upstairs in their bedroom, he turned to my mother with a happy smile. '*What* good company David is!' She would save up these treasures for us, his unintentionally revealing remarks, and we would laugh over them together, but not unkindly. She was still at heart the same young woman who pulled people to pieces because she found them 'so uncommonly interesting, especially their funny little ways'. To be able to laugh gently at my father behind his back was her best, really her *only* way of coping with him. I must have been seventeen or eighteen when I first tentatively began to discuss him with her. Talking over my difficulties, I found to my relief, not only that she was able to understand and sympathise, but that she saw our problem figure in a very similar light.

Father's good fairy had piled gifts upon him in his cradle. She had endowed him with a great many virtues but had left him sadly deficient in one important respect. He had very little sense of humour and, above all, no ability whatever to look at and to laugh at himself. Realising this, my mother never hesitated to take on the job on his behalf; casting herself in the role of court jester to a self-centred and somewhat pompous monarch. Like all good jesters, she knew to a hair's breadth how far to go and she never hurt him;

leaving him, as often as not, blissfully unconscious of the fact that he was being teased. He found her, at times, a puzzling, unpredictable personality and not quite to be trusted; someone whom he never knew *what* she might be saying next. He was able to report her remarks with amusement, as to my brother in the letter about his knighthood, yet betray no sign that her barbs had penetrated. And as he grew older, and honours were heaped upon him, he did become a trifle over-inflated and in need of a helpful prick from Mother's puncturing pin.

He returned from one of his business trips abroad, having met Stephen Spender in the aeroplane. This was exciting news, since we admired the poet immensely. What was he like? we wanted to know. Father was ready to inform us. 'Oh,' he said, 'he has a tremendously high opinion of *me*.' He was not, alas, skilful at delving into personalities or explaining people to people; his self-preoccupation prevented it and our curiosity was seldom satisfied. Occasionally, however, he produced a memorable *mot*. He had sat next to the Queen Mother at a banquet, and we asked him afterwards how they had got on together. She was the easiest of persons; he had experienced no difficulties. We pressed further. 'But what did you say to each other?' 'We talked about dominant women.'

Moral indignation bubbled easily out of him. He was such an earnest man, but his impassioned pronouncements are often hard to take seriously. I have already mentioned his abstinence but have not, so far, touched upon his horror of gambling. 'The sports are on,' he writes from a steamer on his world tour in 1912, 'but as they have turned it into a race-meeting and are taking bets and shouting the odds all the time I have lost any interest I had in the proceedings. Fortunately I had not entered for any of the events. (I was too disgusted at the way things were being run.) Had I done so I should have refused to play off my heats under such conditions. Fancy ladies having their names shouted out by a "booky" as they competed in a potatoe race!'

The year 1949 was one of travel both for my parents and for ourselves. Father's second round-the-world journey, which occupied the winter months, had, I need hardly stress, a serious purpose behind it and in Canada, the United States and New Zealand he was involved in a series of keenly-fought book trade campaigns, needling governments and securing a great deal of useful publicity in his efforts to obtain the freer and wider distribution of British books. He had by this time made himself an emissary for the trade as a whole and, in the later decades of his life, tended to view books in the abstract, as symbols rather than individual titles by specific authors. Although he still put a lot of enthusiasm and hard work into the job of promoting his own publications – we had just published Thor Heyerdahl's best seller *The Kon-tiki Expedition* – this occupied, so to speak, only his left hand. With his right, he was championing broader causes, fighting against unfair tariffs, discriminatory legislation and restrictive import quotas.

Our own journey lasted much longer, for we spent the whole of that formative year travelling from the top to the bottom of Africa. We went there because the eastern side of the continent was coloured pink on the map; hence a part of the sterling area. We wanted to travel and my royalties allowed it, but foreign currency was limited and we could not roam at will in Europe. This was sad for Periwinkle. Until she married me, she had never left the British Isles and she longed for France and Italy. Africa, however, entranced us both. We grew up, to some extent, that year and, when we returned, we found the confined and claustrophobic atmosphere of my parents' house impossible to bear. (How depressing it still seems to me when I look back; the contrast between their stimulating royal progresses round the globe and their stultifying and sombre home routine.) We had become sociable beings in Kenya and the Cape and now, when we stayed in Hampstead, we grew restive; we could not sit evening after evening in the drawing-room, chatting desultorily while my father read *The Times*. One night, after supper, we announced that we were going out. We were driving down to Regent's Park, to drop in on some new friends we had made. Father lowered his paper; my mother stared up from her sewing. 'Going *out*?' Such a move was too radical to be assimilated and they reacted with stunned disbelief.

Periwinkle had now spent sufficient time in my company to have formed her own opinion about my curious states of health. In Switzerland, we had slogged our way up the alps with skins attached to our skis, for I despised the new-fangled mechanical lifts and hoists. In the bamboo forests of the Ruwenzori, in tropical heat, we had toiled for hours up a vertical mountain track upon which she eventually collapsed, too exhausted to struggle any further. She had accompanied me thousands of feet underground, into copper and gold and diamond mines, tramping along endless tunnels and inspecting the various processes. And she had seen me collapsed limply in a chair on a hotel verandah, afflicted for days on end with all the old symptoms; a nervous wreck after the strain of driving hundreds of miles with the car shaken violently and incessantly on corrugated dirt roads.

She made her deductions and, when our travels were over, she urged me to visit again the heart specialist in Harley Street who, thirteen years earlier, on my return from Germany, had given me such a bad report. We went together and, after he had examined me, he asked to see her alone. He was instantly reassuring; indeed, he grew quite lyrical; my organ, apparently, was in splendid shape. All I needed was a dose of confidence. 'Tell him to stop worrying about himself,' were his parting words. We walked happily out into the spring sunshine, bought a bunch of daffodils and took them up to Hampstead. Mother was in the groundfloor kitchen, my father's old study, and we burst in upon her, waving our bouquet. The good news appalled her. She stared at us, aghast. 'Those dark shadows under your eyes,' she said. 'I always thought they were *heart*.'

Out of the journal I kept on our travels I was able to fashion a novel, which was accepted for publication by Michael Joseph. I felt sufficiently established by this time to come out into the open and use my own name. I thought I might get away with it, but unfortunately I was over-confident. Perhaps it would not have mattered had the book caused no ripple, but it was made a Book Society choice and attracted a certain amount of attention. The Society, that year, was celebrating an important anniversary. They gave a party to which, as the author of the current choice, I was naturally invited. And during the course of the evening, one of my hosts took the trouble to make it clear to me that I owed my success entirely to the fact that I was my father's son. There was probably something in what he said, but I still ask myself, need he have said it? And I took comfort from the thought that, however eager they might have been to please the old man, the panel would hardly have saddled the membership with a dull or unreadable book.

My brother, after Oxford, Harvard and his spell in the Navy, was now at Allen & Unwin, concentrating on the trade side and working his way up the ladder I had abandoned after the war. I have always felt guilty at my defection, for by taking my place Rayner sacrificed his own promising career as an author. Even with my slighter and lighter writings, I was aware early on of the impossibility of combining the two careers, but my brother had always intended to retire at an early age and continue with his books. I remember him, perhaps with his relative and namesake Rayner Storr in mind, mentioning 'forty' when we were all together, with the predictable result that the Chairman, after an instant's calculation, announced that *he* would not have retired by then! (In fact, since my father's death, Rayner has – very fortunately for all of us – retained his hold of the helm.)

After Father had completed his first fifty years in the book trade – an event celebrated by booksellers as well as publishers with speeches and presentations in honour of one 'whose name is, without doubt, the most widely known in the trade, not only in this country but in the whole world' – it was decided that his portrait should be painted and Oskar Kokoschka accepted the commission. Since my father was, of course, far too busy a man to sit – and waste time – in an artist's studio, Kokoschka agreed, with great good humour and adaptability, to paint him at work in his office. This necessitated certain preparations. A wooden platform was built for his chair, to raise him a suitable height above his desk, and perched at an unaccustomed altitude he continued for several weeks to dictate his letters, answer phone calls and interview authors while the artist, working in cramped conditions, laboured at his canvas in a corner of the room.

A pair of sharply contrasted characters – what did they have in common, apart from the fact that each, in his own field, had achieved international repute? – the two men reacted splendidly to each other. Kokoschka's habit was to fuel his painting energies with hard liquor, and a bottle of whisky was provided for his consumption when the sittings began. Father himself saw to it that this was replenished, an unprecedented relaxation on his part. O.K. also smoked endlessly and that Father tolerated the smoke-laden atmosphere was certainly a tribute to the artist. Respect warmed into affection on both sides. O.K. delighted in my father's swift sallies and the play of his mind as he conducted his business, and on one occasion, after listening to a more than usually adroit telephonic exchange, he leapt from behind the easel and with a shout of 'I do so *love* you!' gave him an applauding Continental embrace. The portrait certainly shows my father at his most alert.

Now that I had reached my thirties and was making a sufficiently adequate success of my career, we were able to settle down together, if not in intimacy, then in reasonably close accord. I consulted him about my problems and, however busy he was, he would always put his work aside and give me his attention when I called on him at Museum Street. He dealt with my literary properties, made every move for me and was unsparing with his advice.

He saw no reason, I am sure, why we should not remain companions and continue together in the same old easy way, but it was not until the end of his life, and in very different circumstances, that I found myself able to re-create with him something of the atmosphere of those walking tours in Germany when I was a boy of twelve or thirteen. For the moment I was still on the defensive, although my antagonism was tempered, now, by a better understanding of his qualities. I was no longer, as I was in my late teens and early twenties, in revolt. At that time I felt I had to struggle in order to assert my values and survive, and, I still remember with pain a few days I spent tramping with him in the Lake District. I was a disciple of Richard Jefferies, *The Story of my Heart* was my Bible, the colours and shapes of lakes and hills, the march of clouds across the sky, were the sources of my happiness, and I wished to be left free to enjoy them. Father marched by my side, invigorated by the wind and the sunshine, describing with unquenchable enthusiasm business deals of the past; deals in which, after much thrusting and parrying, he had invariably outwitted his opponents. I was not, I regret to say, a responsive audience, but seethed inwardly, resenting the murk of facts and figures which blotted out the beauty I might have been enjoying. And ten years later, when I wrote my first – unpublished – novel, my hero Ian, a sensitive young poet, is, not perhaps surprisingly, at loggerheads with his father, a rich and self-made business man.

> 'As he talked the room seemed to fill gradually with notes and loans, settlements and conversions and bills of exchange. At moments like these John Elliott blew finance like a whale blows vapour, and as a consequence all those about him breathed an impalpable, dust-fine essence; the transubstantiation of a thousand profitable deals.
>
> If his parents were only given to whims; if he indulged occasionally in flights of fancy, Ian sighed, yes, then he could have borne with him patiently. Let him but collect with enthusiasm, be it Italian primitives or Staffordshire figures; let him fling wide the noose of his accumulated wealth and rope in shining race horses and splendid, ocean-going yachts. Let there be gatherings and soirées; pageants and parties, and above all let there be spectacle. Let him from the summit of St Paul's, or better still from a balloon, scatter to the winds a cloud of banknotes; dear God, let him not be afraid to use, to rejoice in and to express himself through his fortune, and how straightforward it would be to forgive him everything! Then let his parent act as he please; cut his son adrift without a penny or abandon him unceremoniously to his fate upon the bottom rung. Ian would still find it in his heart to forgive, to love and to admire.'

Later again, when I had calmed down and grown more confident in myself. I was able to recognise that in business affairs my father was an artist. His mind was sharp and worked swiftly, cutting through tangles to the essentials; this was his knack and he revelled in it and the achievements it brought him. That he was not a visual man, drawing little or no sustenance from the appearance of things, upon which I had always fed, I now realised had to be accepted rather than regretted or railed against. I seemed, at last, to have matured to the extent that I could begin to appreciate his skills.

Nineteen

'In about half an hour's time we are due at Karachi where work starts and I shall probably not prove such a faithful correspondent. At the end of the week we shall leave for Bombay. David is proving a delightful companion as I knew he would.'

It is September 1952 and my father and I are on our way to Tokyo. A mammoth business journey lies ahead. Rayner cannot be spared to accompany him and I have been enlisted in the capacity of secretary and keeper of the journal. Father's optimism, you will notice, is irrepressible as far as his elder son is concerned, but as the weeks go by I sometimes find my appointed role difficult to sustain. At the start, whether through a sense of economy or an urge for close companionship or a mixture of both, he arranges that we shall share a hotel room. This is not a sensible idea and adds to the stresses of what is proving a most demanding journey.

'There is one thing I badly wish I had packed,' he writes to Mother on the plane between Karachi and Bombay, 'and that is one of my *thin* woolly belly bands to wear at night. You might see whether it would cost much to air freight me one (the lightest). Consult Miss Davis [his personal secretary at the office] – she would despatch it for you.'

In the plane between Bombay and Madras the saga continues.

> 'I was a good deal disturbed by "griping" the first two days due entirely to keeping the fan going all night, the first night, with nothing but cotton over my tummy. David feels that he *must* have the fan on all night; I regard it as a menace unless one is covered by some wool. He accordingly got another room just to sleep in. It occurs to me that those body belts of mine I asked you for are

now so ancient that they will be far too small. If you have
not yet posted one will you please measure it first. Meanwhile I fold my little shawl into a long narrow strip which
I lay across the bed at the appropriate point . . .'

Two days later, at the hotel in Madras, he once again returns to
the subject.

'Do you remember that I inherited a red band to fix
round the tummy to cover up the top of one's trousers? It
would be useful here because it is pleasant to have the fans
full blast.'

His needs, I am thankful to say, were finally met in Singapore.

'Thank you for your welcome letter of the 17th and for
the belly band. It is a little tight but serviceable. Travelling
with David is a mixture of Bernard and Johnnie. [My
Unwin and Storr uncles.] He is most particular about
clothes; *must* have a clean shirt *every* day; must have his
clothes constantly pressed etc but a bad sleeper; can't
survive without the fan going hard; upset by the slightest
noise. But he is very sweet and attentive and we get along
admirably.'

These extracts from his letters may suggest that my father was
an hypochondriacal Edward Lear character, a man of puny physique
battling against climatic odds. Let me at once dispel the idea.
Although he was by now approaching seventy, he was still extraordinarily strong and energetic. But he had his foibles and he
fussed about them : draughts were one, damp seats another. (He
had a terror of piles.) There is a charming photograph taken of my
parents at the time of their engagement, sitting side by side on a
garden bench. He has his arm round her shoulders, he is cuddling
her happily, and all is well for he is adequately protected. A sharp
eye can detect, protruding from beneath his trousers, the corner of

a folded newspaper. Has he offered my mother a share of it? Not. I have to admit, as far as can be ascertained.

He *must* have been strong to have survived our astonishing travels. We flew altogether on twenty-eight different aeroplanes; Constellations, Argonauts, decrepit Dakotas. They were all piston-engined and slow by today's standards. The noise level was appalling; you had to shout to be heard, and the continual vibration was very wearing. Staggering down the gangway after an exhausting flight, we would fall into the hands of a reception committee. 'There were four press reporters and photographers to greet our arrival at the airport who peppered me with questions, but despite my repeating three times that it was *paper* that was six times the pre-war price and that books had increased relatively little they quoted me as saying that books were six times the price, which is absurd.' In Pakistan, 'as I anticipated my chief preoccupation *here* is the abolition of the obstacles to the free flow of books. It is New Zealand all over again but the obstacles are accidental and the methods of my campaign rather different. I have been helped on all sides and am to see the Prime Minister tomorrow morning,' while in India, 'I found myself most unexpectedly involved in yet another campaign – this time to prevent books being subjected to a sales tax. It meant making additional calls over and beyond the booksellers and librarians and time was short. But it resulted in our having interesting interviews with the Governor (Bajpai) an outstanding man of remarkable culture with a faultless Oxford accent and the Chief Minister (Moraji Desai) a deeply religious man (largely responsible for the threatened tax) who seemed to regard 90% of books as pernicious.'

We were to meet other Indian panjandrums: Rajagopalachari in Madras, Nehru in New Delhi. On we went, hopping from India to Ceylon to Singapore, across to Indonesia, over to Hong Kong and finally to Tokyo; staying at Residencies and Embassies and entertained by British Council representatives, Trade Commissioners, High Commissioners and Ambassadors. A marvellously interesting, top level, packed and demanding tour. Here is one of my father's typical days.

'My programme here is as usual a very full one. Up at 7, breakfast 7-45, away with the Deputy High Commissioner at 8-30. Visited the British Information Services office and at 9-15 addressed the Dacca publishers and booksellers. Quite an astonishing number. Spoke to them and answered questions until 11-30. Visited a few fifth rate shops; all the good ones being closed for the Muslim holiday. [These would be raised wooden cupboards with the bookseller squatting cross-legged in the middle of his stock. Father was a great one for leaving *no* stone unturned.] Other appointments at 12-45 and 2 pm and lunch in between at the British Council Rep's house. I have a press conference at 4-15, I am to give a lecture at 5 pm; to attend a party at 7-30, a dinner at 8-30 and so it goes on. I have an equally full day tomorrow including a broadcast and we leave Sunday morning for Calcutta.'

In Madras, one afternoon, we had an appointment at a Hindu Cultural Centre, the Bharatiya Vidya Bhavan. Father had published the first of a series of histories for them, *The Vedic Age*. 'We were met on the steps of the big building by quite a deputation and were escorted round the theatre, library, museum etc,' I wrote in my journal. 'Going down one passage we passed the door of a room where thirty or so young girls were having a music and dancing class. They were sitting on the floor, a repeat pattern of glossy black heads and black pigtails, and all their little sandals were lying strewn on the floor outside. We had tea at a long table with all the "high-ups" – Father sitting next to the 84-year-old Vice-President, whom he made roar with laughter by telling him that the most intelligent thing he (father) had done in his life was to choose his parents. They think a lot of the family out here, and this went down well. Father made a little speech and was garlanded. Later, as we were moving out, he very adroitly (by talking about "mere publishers" and "sons who were authors") managed to transfer the said paper garland on to my shoulders and I was left with the problem of dealing with it!'

I managed to squeeze out of most days a fairly full measure of enjoyment. What I came to find wearisome, often reducing me to a state of fretful boredom, was my enforced attendance at my parent's public pronouncements. Father was constantly on his feet. He had about three set pieces with him, which he knew by heart, and they all had interchangeable sections so that he could dismantle them and screw them together, bolting in the essential paragraph to adapt it for local conditions. Asked to address a meeting at no notice, in the middle of a busy day's programme, he would turn up trumps, provided he could talk on a subject connected with the book trade. And I was always at his side. I had to listen to them all. In the end a bug of some kind gripped me by the throat and I went down with a bad attack of bronchitis, lying in bed in the Bengal Club with a loaned servant sleeping outside my door. The British Council had earlier booked me up to address a gathering of school teachers and librarians. As I was incapacitated, rather than disappoint them, my conscientious and over-occupied father came to the rescue and spoke to them instead.

He allowed himself very few breaks; on the whole we kept solidly at it. And this was an advantage, as I explain in a letter to Periwinkle.

> 'I am dazed, not because of the work but because we've just had two days' "holiday", and while I can cope with business plus Father these "pleasure" excursions are appalling from my point of view. We are suddenly stranded alone together, with the common thread snapped. No press interviews and invitations, no people to surround us and keep him happily occupied. We are thrown back on one another and even our bowels, current state of, are invoked as an aid to conversation. He is *exactly* the same man who took me to Germany when I was a child and who drove me nearly scatters when I was a young man.'

On one of our rare half-days off, when we were lent a car to view the local sights,

> 'Luckily we had an American girl with us and she was

useful as a buffer state. I was glad to travel in front and leave Father to make conversation in the back, which consisted of a detailed tirade against the USA in the matter of treatment of books – he is sublimely one-track – which she took quite well on the whole. But thinking back I feel that a certain numbness, a lassitude must have crept over me. All this part of the world is very stuffy and sticky and to fulfil an arduous programme in battering heat tends to absorb your energy. Leaving nothing over for chivalry, I suppose.'

We were co-existing throughout on two quite distinct levels. He was totally occupied, as he always was, in book trade affairs, while I was engaged socially and visually. This was to emerge at the start of our journey.

'Travelling with Father is in a way very interesting because I can understand now exactly where we part company. He induces a sense of isolation, for casual acquaintances do not exist as far as he is concerned and he pays no attention whatever (not a "good morning") to any other passenger on this aeroplane – not that they are particularly exciting but I've contacted one or two and then am at once confronted with the utter impossibility of linking them up with Father! He's all right when it's someone he's *supposed* to be meeting! A fat young doctor-cum-anthropologist has given me his card. He heard us discussing Heyerdahl at Rome airport restaurant and button-holed me afterwards. When S.U. came along and the subject of *Kon-tiki* was mentioned, without in the least melting his deeply suspicious attitude, Father came out, forthright, violently, with "It's a *great* book. A *great* book." The fat doctor stammered and gasped and that was the end of that and though he clung on to me tenaciously, being a talker and travelling single, no further word was addressed him from the Master! But I'm not in the slightest perturbed – we shall be meeting quite enough people – and towards me he is unfailingly kind and thoughtful. I occupy the porthole seat all the time (the only one with a view) and we are doing fine.'

A journey like ours was expensive to fund and was paid for by the firm. Set against the cost of our air fares and accommodation – when we did stay in an hotel we usually put up at the best one available – the extras that ironed out the wrinkles of the day were altogether inconsiderable; trivial sums which I felt should be accepted and paid without quibble. This was *not* how my father felt, and it was on these monetary trifles that he so often fixed his attention.

'He has nearly a thousand pounds here in Japan in blocked currency but is reluctant to use taxis even in Tokyo and will walk miles rather than spend 100 yen (2/-) and if he *has* to, insists on a "small taxi" – uncomfortable little vehicles – because they are a fraction cheaper than the American-car type! I was reprimanded the other day for being over hasty in purchasing a newspaper it turned out we didn't want. Cost : not quite twopence. "Ah, but you've never had difficulty in earning a few pence etc." He should be made to tear up and throw away at least five pounds daily, don't you agree?'

I have already touched upon his ingrained resistance to tipping. But tips were essential in those Asian and eastern countries if willing and cheerful service was desired. Because I could see that all this constant disembursement caused him pain, I suggested that I might take over the tipping myself and spare him the ordeal. Rather to my surprise, he accepted the offer. 'I can only plead,' he was to write later in his autobiography, 'that my instinctive economy on small things, which my elder son often bemoans when we travel together, has made it possible for me to do larger things which I felt more important.' A statement which, given a moment's thought, does not bear analysis. Here he is, at the time, writing to Mother from Tokyo.

'Living here is frightfully expensive – such a contrast with 39 years ago. Even this air letter form costs 1/- instead of 6d elsewhere. We were given a most marvellous Japanese luncheon today which I managed to eat with chopsticks from start to finish and I was shocked to discover afterwards that it must have cost more than £1 each person. Tomorrow we lunch with the Ambassador.'

Twenty-five years earlier, he had been writing to her from New York: 'Prices here are terrible. It shocks my economical mind. I hate *eating* money!'

Twenty

Father went into property, reluctantly and at an unpropitious moment, just before the war. He took the plunge, not from any prospect of financial gain, but to save his tennis court. The seven acres of the Oak Hill Park Estate came up for sale and, fearful that it might be bought and built over, he decided to take action. But 'with the outbreak of war some tenants just left and others flitted overnight, with arreas of rent unpaid. Only a small minority gave due notice and attended to their dilapidations. There came a moment when my wife and I were almost the only residents left in the park. The director in charge retired and I was left to "hold the baby". At this point the War Office stepped in.'

Requisitioning by the military of many of the old houses was to sound the eventual death knell of the Victorian estate. By the end of the war some were in a semi-ruinous condition and the property still continued to involve my father in much annoyance and hard work. Oak Hill Park was an incubus and it was losing money. Then, imperceptibly, the tide began to turn. The crumbling, derelict houses, which nobody wanted to live in, blossomed through the fifties into a prime site for development; a speculator's dream. With the arrival of the sixties, to his surprised relief, he found that he was sitting on a gold mine. His Midas touch had worked again.

He soon had it all fixed up. He would sell the estate to a large firm of contractors, holding back for his own use a half acre site adjacent to the Old Garden, where he would build a smaller and more convenient house and, need it be said, another tennis court. The firm that was to develop the site would be entrusted with the construction of this house at cost price. He had everything sewn up, his and my mother's future assured, and he would be making a lot of money. He turned to us for applause and was very much put out when, instead of clapping hands, Periwinkle and I ventured to be critical. A family debate ensued. Debate is, in fact, a misnomer, for there was no general discussion. We were attempting to argue Father out of doing what he intended to do, which was always a hopeless venture. He was not prepared to be deflected, but we were upset and angry enough to argue just the same.

We wished him to consider converting the original buildings horizontally into flats (they were all, save one, semi-detached) thus preserving the 1851 estate. By no means all the houses were in a ruinous state and they were handsome examples of their period. We told him about a similar exercise in rehabilitation – the Paragon at Blackheath – but he did not want to listen. His mind was already made up. The place was too far gone to be tinkered with and it must all be swept away.

And swept away it duly was, giving place to a drab and characterless assembly of buildings of no architectural or visual interest. A sorry ending. One house does remain standing to point the contrast; my sister's old home, now converted into flats, as we had hoped the others might have been. This house was saved because my father had arranged for her lease to be extended, giving her a few more years in residence while she looked for another place to live. By the time she came to leave the urge for demolition had abated, or perhaps the money had run out.

Father did not make himself popular in Hampstead by selling out to the developers and my mother was 'cut' by acquaintances when she went shopping in the village. She had not questioned his action for she never interfered in his business life; she did not consider this to be any concern of hers. So although the affair touched her nearly, she sounded no note of criticism and acquiesced without comment in the destruction of the estate. The appearance of their ultra-modern new house took her by surprise; she told me she had expected something with 'long windows'. (One assumes neo-Georgian. Had no one shown her an elevation?) And it turned out, too, to be a great deal larger than she had anticipated, but this was my father's responsibilty, for in answer to the architect's request for measurements, he had run a tape over the substantial rooms he was accustomed to living in.

His new court was laid down first, for the old one almost instantly disappeared into the foundations of a block of flats, and for the best part of a year he played his games below the concrete shell of his future home. Because he had driven too hard a bargain and given the builder no incentive to exert himself, work proceeded at a snail's pace and the building, when finally completed, proved full of faults. However, my parents adjusted well to their new life. Father once again had a study of his own and my mother came to like the wall-sized sliding windows in the living-room. They opened on to a south-facing terrace where, on fine days, she would sit in the sun above the caged red desert of the tennis court.

When the move up the road became imminent, they had to decide what furniture to take with them. Top of my mother's list of pieces to be jettisoned was the massive pianola, that had taken up its position beside the door into the drawing-room in the late 1920s and had never shifted since. Father's fingers might have grown a little stiff over the years, but he could still pedal. Get rid of the pianola? He was shocked at the idea. He informed her, quite seriously, that he would need it to play on in the evenings, *after she had gone.*

This, alas, was hubris, for in due course he was to conform to the statistics and die before her. (They were born in the same year.) Fit all his life, with a slow pulse and spare physique, neither smoking nor drinking, taking regular exercise and playing a vigorous game of tennis into his late seventies, never walking when he could trot and always leaping upstairs two or three steps at a time, my father had unbounded confidence in his longevity. *His* parents had been long-lived. Modern science should be able to see him through to his century. But the proverbial small cloud on the horizon was to make itself apparent soon after they moved from the old house. The first symptoms of diabetes showed themselves, the disease that, over the next decade, was to sap his strength, weaken his eyesight and dissipate his energies.

Before we treat of this, let us consider him again in springy health. There was the moment when my mother, finding herself in the neighbourhood, decided to call on him at the office. She was about to cross Museum Street when he erupted out of the front door of Ruskin House and, holding the flap of his double-breasted coat firmly across his chest, began to trot briskly in her direction. He was not expecting to see her, he was busy with his thoughts, and had swept by and was receding into the distance before she could pull herself together and turn and call after him – in vain. He was moving fast and already out of earshot.

Another bizarre episode I remember well, for I was living at home at the time. We were at dinner in the basement one evening, some question or other came up and a book was needed to answer it. Father knew the whereabouts of every book in the place, and the volume we wanted was at the top of the house. He instantly leapt from the table, catapulted himself in his standard manner up the three tall flights of stairs, found the book and raced down again, resuming his place with his breathing only slightly modified. We thought no more of the incident until later, when my parents entered their bedroom on the first floor. Here a strange sight presented itself. One of the sash windows had been flung up and remained wide open and on the bed lay the inlaid wooden box in which my mother kept her jewels; hacked about and badly splintered, but with the lid still locked. Father's innocent dash up the stairs in search of information had disturbed a burglar on the job!

I wintered in Morocco with a writer friend in 1959, and while making our way down to the warmer southern half of the country we called in at a rather gloomy seaside hotel north of Casablanca, where my parents were staying for a fortnight's holiday. I may well have suggested Morocco to them, as I intended going there myself, but their choice was disastrous; we found them marooned in an out-of-season, modern and hideous resort.

Our arrival stimulated them and Father sparkled entertainingly. Henry was staggered by the punch he packed. He was the human equivalent of at least forty arabs, he told me as we were leaving the hotel. Mother too, was in good form. Under a grey sky, in cool air, we walked on the damp, deserted sands where, instead of shells and seaweed, flabby condoms lay in the foam along the water's edge. In her youth, she would have reacted prudishly. In late middle-age she had grown robust. 'Well, at least they're a sign of *life*,' she said, and flicked at them with the ferrule of her stick.

Throughout the sixties, my father was to battle with his disease. At first they were light skirmishes; the enemy was beaten back without much difficulty and lurked cowering in foxholes, always, however, to return to the attack. His weapons were medicines, a rigorous diet and his inflexible will. He tested himself regularly and continued almost exactly as he had always done. One concession was forced on him. Failing eyesight was making it hard for him to drive and he now had a chauffeur; or is this too dignified a description, implying a full-time person in a uniform? His driver took him to the office each morning, worked at Allen & Unwin in some practical capacity during the day, and drove him home again in the evening. He was most certainly not at my mother's beck and call. Since Father was a staunch upholder of the National Health Service – he had paid his contributions over the years and believed in getting his money's worth – he would be driven in state to the surgery, where he would join the queue and wait for an hour, or perhaps even longer, while his chauffeur sat outside in the car, thus frittering away not only his own time but his employee's as well. We hinted that a private appointment might be justified in his case, but he did not agree. And on an earlier occasion, when he had had trouble with an ulcer on the tip of one of his ears and surgery was advised, he could have paid to have had this carefully and aesthetically done. Instead, he chose to have the small operation 'on the Service' and suffered a barbarous National Health snip, which did not improve his appearance but left him unruffled.

Apart, then, from the luxury of a driver, the programme of his life remained unmodified. A glance over the journeys he made during these years will underline the scale of his activities. In addition to his annual visit to the Frankfurt Book Fair, in 1961 he was visiting publishers and booksellers in Israel and Turkey, and the following year he attended the International Publishers Congress in

Spain. In 1963 he travelled extensively in East and Central Africa and in 1965 – he was by now over eighty – he went off, on his own, to Mexico and the United States. At the end of this long and arduous journey he was in Washington, playing an active role in another international congress. He must have been among the last of his generation still on their feet at these professional junketings; most of his contemporaries, one would guess, would have long since thankfully retired.

'I sometimes despair of getting another letter written to you,' he informs my mother at this time. 'I seem to be kept so continually on the go, and such a flood of invitations to receptions and cocktail parties keep pouring in, calling for immediate attention. I got up at an early hour this morning to try to cope with them. I forget where my last letter left off. I think I was on my way to a Hawaiian Banquet and concert. It was quite interesting but I was glad to be a trifle deaf. You would have been blasted out of the hall. The concert went on too long and it was nearly midnight before I got to bed.

This morning I had to speak on the "manufacturing clause" in the new American Copyright Act and when I had done so I received quite an ovation. The session lasted so long that we were all late for the big Readers' Digest lunch, and the lunch made us late for the afternoon session on the "free flow of books" at which I had to propose a resolution on behalf of the Publishers' Association concerning the Florence agreement. Storer was able to follow it up with a dramatic intervention – a letter from the President to Congress urging prompt action.'

After a conference with the Belgian delegation about their French /Flemish troubles he went on to 'an excellent party where substantial refreshments were served,' and 'at 8 pm we left by bus for a Rodeo show. Cowboys riding bucking horses and bucking bulls bareback, lassooing etc. It was a long drive but quite an amusing show of the circus type. Tomorrow we are to spend the day on a boat trip on the Potomac River and afterwards to a reception at the British Embassy. I have thus far kept remarkably well and appear to be less fatigued than most people. I suppose that I am more hardened to this kind of activity.'

His refusal to modify his life and to adjust to his increasing infirmities brings me into the story again. He had to be in Stockholm on business in the summer of 1967 and he planned to take a short holiday afterwards. But he really had become too old and frail to be allowed to wander off by himself and, as even *he* recognised his need for a companion, I flew out to join him.

I found him still flogging himself along in his accustomed style. With a Swedish friend we toured the sights of Stockholm and then did the same thing all over again in Uppsala, after which we travelled on by ourselves into central Sweden.

'Here there is only *one* monument within reach,' I tell mother. 'An old church, and we saw it this morning. So we are left with the pine woods, the calm lake and the white and gleaming birches. All wide open and vast and empty. I can *feel* the breath of the polar ice cap just sitting up there to the north of us and hope and hope that the sun will go on shining. The nights are so short that I haven't noticed them yet. I suppose it does get darkish for an hour or so. Father is in very good form. He is eating well and supper at 6-30 pm suits him down to the ground. We *both* tested ourselves last night and came out much the same colour (rather like this ink) which pleased him greatly. Everyone dresses most formally in this country, even out here in the wilds. All the men (except me) wore white shirts and bow ties and smart suits to breakfast, which pleased Pa no end as he hadn't got round to unpacking and he was *de rigueur* in his lounge suit!'

But his physical deterioration saddened me. He had lost his old bounce and when we went for our little pottering walks along the lakeside paths, he stumbled a lot; the toes of his shoes knocking into the roots that snaked above the ground. His sight, too, had become muzzy and uncertain and he could not distinguish distant objects. Still, he enjoyed himself in a quiet way and returned to England refreshed by the interlude. My job as male-nurse-companion had not proved arduous; indeed, his more subdued, less vehement, elderly persona was easier to get on with. For the first time in our lives together our roles were reversed, and how odd I felt it. I was now by far the stronger and the more active. For a change, *I* was looking after *him*.

Twenty-One

I am sitting in my bedroom at the Hotel Gemsli in Thusis, reading a book by Italo Svevo. Svevo, curiously enough, is describing the death of his father. Three minutes walk away up the hill, in a room in a big modern hospital, my father is lying unconscious. He is gravely ill. I walk up there every day and sit by his bedside, but we cannot communicate. He has gone a long way away from me and he may well be dying. There is nothing I can do. I can only hang on and hope for the best.

Fifteen months have passed since our last journey, and it is the end of September 1968. We are in Switzerland together to satisfy an ambition, an aspiration that has nagged him over many years. He has been anxious to visit a particular valley, the Fex valley, above Sils-Maria in the Engadine, a place praised by one of his authors whom he most admired and who was a friend : Galsworthy Lowes Dickinson. This was our objective and we achieved it, but at what a cost ! The village was too high; the season too late. The expedition was thoroughly ill-judged.

'The holiday is not going quite to plan, I'm afraid,' I inform my mother in a letter begun at Tiefencastel and continued at Thusis. (This is the understatement of the year, but I am doing my best not to be alarmist. She is now bedridden; the previous autumn she had a fall and broke a hip and the bone has not yet mended.)

'The altitude at Sils, coupled with the exercise he was taking, finally had a bad effect on him. I am afraid that to attempt the old things – walks in the mountains and so on – was *not* a good idea and I paid more attention to his *mental* health – ie keeping him cheerful and happy, with a feeling that he was achieving something along the old lines – than to his physical state. Of course it was not the ideal place. Any worth-while walk involved climbing and the distances between the little restaurants were too great. There were few days when it was possible to sit comfortably in the open. I kept pressing Locarno or Lugano – buses went there direct from Sils – but you know how impossible it is to get him to alter a plan, once made. He's (alas) far from flexible.'

The journey out had been a nightmare, with floods on the way to London Airport, a missed plane, and the next taking off an hour later than scheduled. And he had seemed so alarmingly small and fragile among the thronging crowds; so insecure on his feet that I expected at any moment to have him barged into and laid flat by a carelessly swung piece of luggage. At Zürich we had to take a bus to the railway station and catch a train to Chur, and at Chur we had to change trains to continue on to St Moritz. By this time it was completely dark. We arrived at St Moritz at 9-40 pm to find that – I quote from my father's letter – 'the last bus had left about three hours earlier and we had to resort to a taxi costing SW frcs 29 (nearly £3)'. He was exhausted when we reached the hotel. The management had confused our bookings and he found himself 'with a double bed and a sitz bath and rather cramped quarters. The only switch we could find in the bathroom in the dark did not work, which was discouraging, and when I opened my attaché case I found my jar of diabetic jam smashed. I was so tired and exasperated that I went to bed without stopping to unpack. A huge "pudding" to cover you and nothing satisfactory round your neck.'

Next morning we found that, although the gardens of the châlets still blazed with cheerful colours, drivers were scraping the frost off their windscreens in the hotel car park. At 6000 feet, winter felt just round the corner. As the days went by the weather remained fitful, the sun made rare appearances, the sky was never clear and it was impossible to keep warm. Father's pace had slowed to a crawl and to restore my circulation I had to dash ahead and run round in circles like a dog. He was in almost constant pain and functioned only by incessantly dosing himself with pills. He seldom mentioned his discomfort and behaved with great courage.

> 'I wish for David's sake that I could walk like I used to. I seem to be able to do so little without my tablets. They are a Godsend and no doubt I shall do better.'

The next day he writes more optimistically.

> 'I have indeed done infinitely better with the aid of 4 tablets (my tennis ration for these days). We followed David's less steep way up into the Fex Valley and we were both enchanted by the scenery. When we got near the top of the ridge it was all so beautiful that we decided to carry on. To my surpise my legs carried me on up and there were plenty of seats on which to rest. Eventually, we dropped down to the first little village where we both enjoyed portions of coffee and David some bacon and eggs. As I had more walking ahead of me and was not hungry, I found one lightly boiled egg sufficient. To show you how expensive life here is owing to a Swiss franc costing 2/- that meagre repast ran us into 21/-. The way down was through a beautiful gorge and it made quite a long round for one so out of practice. We must have been walking for nearly 4 hours. It has quite renewed my confidence. I am devoutly thankful I brought my stick, I don't know how I should have managed without it. Sorry I did not bring my mittens. With my Norfolk suit plus waistcoat plus Jaeger pants, warm shirt, vest and light overcoat I keep reasonably warm.'

He loved to encounter other not-quite-so-elderly walkers on our excursions, when he would break into fluent German, astonish them by mentioning his age, and reminisce about past exploits, but we had our most interesting encounter in the dining-room of the hotel.

A fellow guest was suddenly crouching beside our table, almost on his knees, so overwhelmed, so delighted was he to have recognised and to be able to greet Sir Stanley. Father, who liked to masticate thoroughly and digest his meals in peace, gave him, I felt, a slightly cool welcome. He told me afterwards, off-handedly, that he had saved his life. He was a German-Jewish bookseller whose permit to stay in England had expired. Despite every effort, and although a job was waiting for him at Bumpus' Bookshop, he had failed to get it renewed. Quite by chance, on the day that Father heard about the case, he was lunching at his club with two Liberal MPs. He interested them, strings were pulled, and the bookseller remained in England. This was just before the war, when an enforced return to Germany would almost certainly have meant the gas chamber.

He survived, up at Sils, for about a week before the collapse. Here is the laconic, modified description (for my mother's benefit) of an extremely harrowing day :

'I always checked most carefully each morning and asked how he was feeling and he seemed none the worse. But on Monday morning I found he had had a rotten night and was feeling none too good. He kept in bed for breakfast and lunch, but in the afternoon we decided it would be best to go straight down to Tiefencastel. I got a comfortable taxi and we had a slow drive over the Julier and I put him to bed on arrival. But it became clear that he was not going to sleep and I called in a doctor. He was extremely efficient and helpful, told Pa he must go into hospital at once for a few days, got him up and into his car and drove us both to the Klinic in Thusis. I left him there in good hands, returning with the doctor to Tiefencastel. I have just packed up his things and my own and am about to follow by the 10 am train.'

We had planned an excursion up another valley for that Monday and, so anxious was he not to upset the arrangement, that he urged me to leave him in bed and set out on the walk by myself. When

I explained that *he* was my primary responsibility and that I could not possibly entertain such a suggestion, relief was written on his face. He looked rotten. His breathing was wheezy and asthmatic and he was in a lot of pain. The car drive over the high pass was testing and I wondered at the time if he would survive it, but I had no choice; I knew I must get him down to a lower altitude as fast as possible and it seemed essential to press on.

Now we had arrived; he was in medical care and responsibility was lifted from my shoulders. I had a breathing space. The doctors at the Krankenhaus were reassuring; he was totally exhausted, they told me, but they were sure he would rally. I paid my statutory call in the morning and another in the late afternoon, and in between, to distract myself, I began to explore the neighbourhood.

Thusis had always been, from Lenzerheide days, the 'town on the other side'. From the top of the ridge, in winter, it could be seen far below, sprinkled over its deep valley floor; so much further down than our resort that a yellowish smog discoloured the snows and it seemed at the bottom of a pit. I had always thought it looked a dull and unpleasant place. On close inspection, I found it very far from dull. The town was strategically placed at the gates of the Via Mala – that awful crack in the rocks, filled with a roaring, boulder-strewn torrent, through which, it is said by some, Hannibal had forced his elephants – and the area around was littered with castles. Some stood boldly on their alps, others grew out of craggy precipices, still others were buried deep in fir woods; lost, romantic, decaying vestiges of an uneasy past. I must have walked and scrambled to ten or a dozen, thinking all the time what a shame it was that he was lying there in hospital and how *he* would have enjoyed them; a little more anxious than I, perhaps, about taking the right path and readier to consult the map; certainly keeping a firmer eye on his watch, but in his own way revelling in the experience.

He surfaced on the third day. I could see that he was conscious but he did not recognise me; was not aware, even, that I was sitting by his bed. But he continued to strengthen and next day I was able to write cheerfully to mother.

'A twinkle in the eye again and the most seraphic smiles. But he doesn't want the effort of talking and conversation is one-sided; quite right. He appreciates my presence and absorbs my news.'

Now I was able to play a more active role and spent much time

'spooning ham and tomatoes and cheese and grapes into him. He has great difficulty in swallowing and things stay around in his mouth for minutes at a time before he can get them down. When he finally *does* make it, he always gives the same rather tired, slightly exasperated grunt. He made me laugh. You put a grape in, there is a great deal of munching, and then suddenly a pip appears, very neatly, between his lips, for me to remove – it was like dealing with a baby bird. I think he is really glad to relax utterly and completely. A total abandonment. He had worn himself to a frazzle, keeping up the mountain-striding, energetic, youthful eighty-three-year-old. This may help him to adjust his perspective. But I don't know. Once he gets his vigour back, he'll probably return to his old form ! !'

At last, the turning point. 'A wonderful moment when at 5-15 pm he suddenly said, "What's the time?" very earnestly, as if it mattered and he had an urgent appointment. After letting the best part of a week slip by without noticing it ! And a little later, nodding at dear old Herr Guetsch in the next door bed. "What's *his* trouble?" Curiosity about something outside his own body; a terrific sign of life.'

From then on, he made slow but steady progress. He was weak, of course, and sadly emaciated; his legs and arms all joints and bones. I had grown accustomed to his appearance, but there was a moment when he was sitting on the commode in his white hospital nightshirt and a peasant girl, a grandchild perhaps of father's fellow patient, came into the room. Her gasp of shocked, slightly hysterical laughter, quickly smothered, hurt me. He was locked into himself and unaware of her reaction, but it upset me to think that life could have done this to him; that such an exceptional man as he should be reduced by age and illness to the semblance of a clown; a risible object in the eyes of a gauche young girl. But this stage passed and he was soon his quicksilver self again, able to put on his clothes and sit on a chair, his tie, as always, neatly clasped with a gold and opal ring, sporting, as always, in his lapel a tiny silver tennis raquet complete with pearl tennis ball, the gift of an admirer in Japan. The nurses loved him. They would gather round while he conversed with them in German, and he would take his large alarm watch out of his pocket and show it off, telling them that it had been four times round the world with him.

The doctors were pleased; he had made a splendid recovery. They pronounced him fit and told him he could travel home. We drove to Zürich airport, a wheeled chair was waiting for him at each end of the journey and, for a change, we flew first class. We went up to Hampstead, he saw my mother, and I took him down to University College Hospital where he was to spend the next few days. He did not much care for this arrangement and thought it unnecessary, but conditions at home were still topsy-turvy, with Mother in bed in the living-room, and tests and a routine check-up were called for. He was a little disgruntled when I went in to say goodbye to him, and no wonder. He must have had enough of hospitals.

Periwinkle was staying with friends in the Algarve and the following day I flew down to join her, reassured that all was now well, that we had pulled him through. But my stay in Portugal was unhappily a brief one. Two days later a cable reached me. He was dead.

Twenty-Two

The self-certainty of my father's generation was perhaps their most remarkable feature. Decision-making was their province; they did not feel the necessity for consultation or discussion. Writing – and thinking – about my life has brought home to me the degree in which I was a pawn on my father's chess board, moved from square to square in accordance with the dictates of his strategy. In spite of his protestations to the contrary, I am sure he would have continued to organise me if I had given him the opportunity to do so. His pressures forced me against my wishes into the role of rebel; a mild one to be sure, but then to be rebellious was not really in my nature. We all escaped in our different ways: my brother into the Navy and University before he entered the firm and my sister into an early marriage, while I was fortunate to find my metier and make myself financially independent as a very young man. In my case, this certainly cleared away obstacles which might otherwise have proved insuperable.

I was fortunate, too, in my mother who kept a sympathetic watch over the situation and in whom I could – and did – confide. Early in 1939 my parents had staying with them on a visit from New Zealand one of my father's brothers, a surgeon, and his youngest (doctor) son. Mother wrote to me in Geneva:

'Peter is looking for a job and I think he is feeling a bit unsettled, not knowing what he is going to do. It's a pity you are not here because you would have many points in common just now. Dear Uncle Will is all agog to help him, and started off rushing him here, there and everywhere, and poor old Peter got quite fed up and wants to manage his own affairs and go his own pace. It's all been very instructive to me and I suppose it's always the same in every family. I feel sorry for both sides, it is so difficult for parents to know the right moment to drop the protective attitude. The running of the child's career is in their hands from babyhood and then suddenly they find they are not wanted and their status and experience in their professions does not count, and I can understand a boy with any spunk naturally wanting to make his own way, without his father's reflected glory ! ! I think the great thing is to try not to *hurt* the older generation, and that is why I think it's best that fathers and sons are not too much together at these stages when difficulties arise. Peter is feeling just like you, a little overshadowed.'

I was growing up under an oak; father had the answer to everything. Doubts seldom assailed him and when he was in any sort of difficulty he was able to resort to prayer. He would take the problem to bed with him, assured that he would wake in the morning with the solution : about this he was completely confident. The Almighty, apparently, never let him down. In turn – as did hundreds of others – I relied on *him*, and when he died his departure tore a hole in my life's fabric. I found myself bereft; standing suddenly alone, without a hand-hold, and instinctively, like a tendril of ivy, I began to grope around for another support. I found it hard to come to terms with the idea that life's practical and business decisions must now be made without him. At the same time and paradoxically, mixed with my sorrow and sense of loss, I was aware of a feeling of relief. It was as if a cloud had lifted and the horizon had cleared. I was free to take off without thought and without questioning my conscience. I was fifty years old, the final barrier had been removed and there was nothing to stop me now from at all times being totally and thoughtlessly myself.

That I should feel this slight but exciting surge of liberty reflects, I am sure, upon my upbringing. Father was loving but he was an autocrat, and he remained an autocrat until the end. Mother, too, after she had recovered from the shock of his death, blossomed wonderfully during the three years which were left to her. Her life became at once more social and more cheerful and grandchildren flocked to the house to enjoy her company, as certain of their welcome and of her embracing love as I had been as a child when visiting *her* mother. Father in old age was a little too formidable, althogether too austere a character, to provide a warm enough ambience for the young, and his presence had tended to frighten them away.

The love and regard I received from him as a boy was, of course, of inestimable value and gave me an inner confidence – possibly misplaced or, at all events, exaggerated – of my own worth which has assisted me all my life. Friends not so fortunate, with unhappy or unsatisfactory childhoods behind them, when they were neglected or starved of necessary affection, envy me this trait. 'You're so lucky, you're so *well-adjusted!*' is a cry that has followed me down the years. But as I grew up, the struggle to find and assert myself, which began in my adolescence and continued on into my twenties, brought me on occasion near foundering point. Towards the end of the war I was in a condition of what was, fairly obviously, nervous collapse; beset by irrational fears and unable to cope with quite normal physical demands. Periwinkle remembers me on a railway platform in a state bordering on terror, and I think it is probable that if I had not had her support, and the support of my mother, I might have slid over the edge and suffered a mental as well as a physical breakdown.

Father was such a *vehement* man. His demands and pressures were at all times fierce and emphatic; if he objected to anything he did so with passion, and this made him tiring to live with and alarming to challenge. He possessed what I can only describe as a pulverising quality. His contemporaries felt it, but they could escape him. I was locked into his orbit; circling him endlessly like a planet round a sun, unable to spin off into my own area of space. This did me no harm as a child, when as Super-Nanny he focused his attention on every insignificant detail of my daily routine; indeed, he taught me many valuable lessons. On one of our walking tours in Germany, when my feet began to hurt, I recollect him standing over me while I removed my shoes and stockings. A shocking sight was revealed; my toes were a bloody mess. Why? *I had forgotten to cut my nails!* Never shall I forget his outburst of indignation and disgust. He made me feel a moral leper and so impressed was I by my turpitude that I have paid, since then, particular and meticulous attention to this essential chore.

Later, I resented his criticisms, took them badly and when I could fought back. Our engagements were trivial but abrasive and they roughened our relationship. We would both have been better without them. For example, as a young man I usually went to bed after my parents, and occasionally I forget to switch off the landing light. Always the first into the bathroom in the morning, Father would discover it still burning and I would be reprimanded at breakfast for thoughtlessly adding to the household bills. After this had happened a few times, I calculated the cost of one 40 watt bulb burning for six or seven hours and, when he next attacked me, laid a halfpenny upon his plate. This was one of my few triumphs – which is perhaps why I remember it! – for he never tackled me on the subject again.

*

Father tended to think, write and talk anecdotally, absorbing his stories and fables from all about him and swiftly making them his own. He was quite unselfconscious about this, never hesitating to bring out a notebook and pencil to jot down a joke which had taken his fancy. On our journeys together I have frequently listened while my (sometimes trivial) observations were served up to strangers and, after a suitable time-lag, have even had them played back to me! He was not, in a social sense, original, rarely if ever switching points or providing surprises but proceeding confidently forward along the well laid and excellently maintained track of his repertoire. Thus, to brief acquaintances, he could sparkle mercurially, and what did it matter, when you did not know him too well, that his gleams of wit and observation were, for the most part, the products of other minds?

The fund of his own tales, stemming back to his world tour as a young man, must serve as an exception to this rule; when strangers who had won his confidence were regaled with spicy histories, all too familiar to his nearest and dearest, who knew them by heart. The lady who was 'carried on board each night, dead drunk, by natives' was a perennial favourite with us all and her charm has not faded.

To those who were close to him he was, perhaps, predictable; but because he was predictable he was dependable, and his dependability inspired loyalty, both from his authors and from his staff at the office. He was a man to be trusted; a man incapable of a mean or underhand action; a man who would never let you down. He was also very ready indeed to know what was best for others, and it was this aspect of his personality which made him difficult to treat with. I cannot do better by way of illustration than to borrow a story from my cousin's most revealing book :

> 'Sir Stanley was an Englishman who never hesitated to go out into the midday sun. A colleague recalls one blistering afternoon in Nigeria when our chief triumphantly located some little bookseller who owed the firm £25. S.U. had been hoping to collect it, but the poor man proved to be in a desperately low state of health, having suffered elephantiasis and only recently survived a serious operation, so that his one-man business had suffered accordingly. Touched by the extreme difficulty of his situation, S.U. agreed to cancel not the *whole* of the debt but £20 of it.
>
> "But why," asked his colleague, when they had made their hot and sticky way back to the hotel, "didn't you cancel the whole amount while you were about it?"
>
> "Ah," said our Chief. "I did not think I had the moral *right* to release the man of all sense of obligation to us, so I thought it better to leave £5 still for him to pay." '

This, surely, is an example of the effect upon him of his strict Nonconformist upbringing and reflects a typically puritanical concern for other peoples' souls. During his youth, he had Congregational ideals and ethics drilled into him. Thanks to his training, this was the mould in which he was cast. Morally upright, a 'good' man in every sense of the word, he had no instinct for religion and his thinking, when he could distract his mind from his business preoccupations, was unoriginal and tended to be a culling from other men's thoughts. That he had no profound, deep-rooted or urgent views on the subject is disingenuously revealed in his autobiography. When asked to contribute to a broadcast series, 'This I believe,' he had seldom, he tells us, faced a more difficult task. *'After two whole weekends of thought on the subject'* (my italics) he managed to write a short credo, a few paragraphs in length, which reads like an anthology.

A much earlier letter to my mother, written before they were married, confirms my feeling that his belief was an enfolding carapace; a shell which enclosed him, rather than an instinctive growth outwards from a spiritual centre:

> 'Our lives are the living expression of our faith, not the faith we hold but the faith that holds us. There is a vast difference between what we profess, or to put it more kindly, what we honestly *think* we believe and the belief that governs our lives. It is the difference between the outward and the inward acceptance of Christianity. Eg; I hold the belief that it is always best to "turn the other cheek," but to my sorrow the belief often fails to hold me!'

*

There was a failure of love in our relationship, but it was on my side only. His love for me did not waver. I often think how sad it must have been for him when I began to distance myself and grow critical and unfriendly. He could not have understood that his personality was an enclosing thicket out of which I had to hack my way, and in my efforts to escape I must at times have been unnecessarily unkind.

We were extraordinarily close to each other until I was in my mid-teens. Perhaps unhealthily close. After his death a stiff brown envelope emerged from among his papers. He had written my full name on the front but on the flap was the seal of an insurance company, for it was obviously a spare envelope which, in the Unwin 'waste not, want not' tradition, he had pressed into use. Inside was a letter I had written to him from boarding school (and had totally forgotten about) together with a brief explanatory line of his own.

'My dearest David,
            Now that I have "passed on" I want you to know how much I appreciated the enclosed and what a comfort it was at the time. It displays your remarkable sensitivity.
                        Your grateful
                            "Daddy." '

Driving home from the office on a dark and drizzly December evening in 1934, my father had had the misfortune to knock down an elderly woman who was crossing the road. She had subsequently died in hospital. This was a terrible thing to have happened and he was profoundly shaken and upset. My overwrought reaction gives, I think, an indication of the strong emotional link that had been forged between us. Here is an extract from my letter.

'My own darling Daddy,
            I feel I must write to you, if only this short note, before we meet again. I don't think you can realize my feelings, I can't put them into words. It is in a way more pleasant to think that the dear old lady would not have lived for many years more, and that her husband will soon follow her. But darling, it might have been any-one, it does seem cruel that you were the one chosen. I have prayed that you may have the courage to bear this catastrophe bravely . . . I somehow feel I ought not to have written this, and yet as we both love each other so greatly, there is such a bond between us, that what hurts

you, hurts me too, and perhaps you would feel a little encouraged . . . God bless you all, the dear lady now resting
peacefully, her husband, you, and God help Mummy also,
so that she may be a source of cheerfulness and inspiration
to you.

            From your own dear son . . .'

After he had died I, too, had the comfort of a great many
sympathetic and understanding letters. An acquaintance in the
'trade' had once sat next to him in great awe at a dinner of the
Society of Bookmen and remembered seeing him at the Frankfurt
Book Fair 'looking very frail but operating with about ten thousand
times as much vigour and know-how as all the showy young men
put together. I thought he would live for ever.'

And he continued : 'When I went into publishing just after the
war the first thing I was made to do (by Rupert Hart-Davis) was
to read *The Truth about Publishing*. And it still seems to me that
whatever truths I have managed to assimilate about the whole
strange business are somehow tinged by your father's personality.
During my professional life he really seemed to constitute single
handed the world of books. I mourn his disappearance.'

'Well, perhaps it was better that it should happen like that,' a
close friend wrote, 'but none the less it can't lessen the shock of
your father's death for you. What a remarkable man he was –
maddening I imagine at times but even from only knowing him
from his public image and from that one meeting one got the
immediate impact of a real 20,000 volt personality. I imagine
that one could say that there was no one remotely like him – quite
a Dad to have.'